The Complete Guide to

POTTY TRAINING CHILDREN

New Sure-Fire Strategies that Make it Easy for Them (and You)

Melanie Williamson

The Complete Guide to Potty Training Children:

New Sure-Fire Strategies that Make it Easy for Them (and You)

Copyright © 2013 by Atlantic Publishing Group, Inc.
1210 SW 23rd Place • Ocala, Florida 34471 • 800-814-1132 • 352-622-1875 Fax
Website: www.atlantic-pub.com • Email: sales@atlantic-pub.com
SAN Number: 268-1250

Author: Melanie Williamson

ISBN 13: 978-1-60138-565-9

Williamson, Melanie, 1981-
The complete guide to potty training children : new sure-fire strategies that make it easy for them (and you) / Melanie Williamson.
   p. cm.
 Includes bibliographical references and index.
 ISBN-13: 978-1-60138-565-9 (alk. paper)
 ISBN-10: 1-60138-565-X (alk. paper)
1. Toilet training. I. Title.
HQ770.5.W55 2012
649'.62--dc23
                    2011042492

BOOK PRODUCTION DESIGN: T.L. Price • design@tlpricefreelance.com

Printed in the United States

A few years back we lost our beloved pet dog Bear, who was not only our best and dearest friend but also the "Vice President of Sunshine" here at Atlantic Publishing. He did not receive a salary but worked tirelessly 24 hours a day to please his parents.

Bear was a rescue dog who turned around and showered myself, my wife, Sherri, his grandparents Jean, Bob, and Nancy, and every person and animal he met (well, maybe not rabbits) with friendship and love. He made a lot of people smile every day.

We wanted you to know a portion of the profits of this book will be donated in Bear's memory to local animal shelters, parks, conservation organizations, and other individuals and nonprofit organizations in need of assistance.

– Douglas & Sherri Brown

PS: We have since adopted two more rescue dogs: first Scout, and the following year, Ginger. They were both mixed golden retrievers who needed a home.

Want to help animals and the world? Here are a dozen easy suggestions you and your family can implement today:

- *Adopt and rescue a pet from a local shelter.*
- *Support local and no-kill animal shelters.*
- *Plant a tree to honor someone you love.*
- *Be a developer — put up some birdhouses.*
- *Buy live, potted Christmas trees and replant them.*
- *Make sure you spend time with your animals each day.*
- *Save natural resources by recycling and buying recycled products.*
- *Drink tap water, or filter your own water at home.*
- *Whenever possible, limit your use of or do not use pesticides.*
- *If you eat seafood, make sustainable choices.*
- *Support your local farmers market.*
- *Get outside. Visit a park, volunteer, walk your dog, or ride your bike.*

Five years ago, Atlantic Publishing signed the Green Press Initiative. These guidelines promote environmentally friendly practices, such as using recycled stock and vegetable-based inks, avoiding waste, choosing energy-efficient resources, and promoting a no-pulping policy. We now use 100-percent recycled stock on all our books. The results: in one year, switching to post-consumer recycled stock saved 24 mature trees, 5,000 gallons of water, the equivalent of the total energy used for one home in a year, and the equivalent of the greenhouse gases from one car driven for a year.

Dedication

This book is dedicated to Natalie, Allison, and Katelyn. They are my constant inspiration.

Acknowledgments

I would like to thank all the parents who helped
me through potty training and contributed
to this book either directly or indirectly.

Table of Contents

Chapter 3: The Preparation 75

Chapter 4: Teaching Toilet Etiquette..... 111

Chapter 5: The One-Day Potty Party Method 123

Chapter 8: Stress-Free Methods of Potty Training 169

Chapter 9: Early Potty Training Methods............................ 181

Chapter 10: Dealing With a Reluctant Child 199

Chapter 11: The Nighttime Bed-Wetting Issue 215

Chapter 12: Common Medical Concerns 227

Chapter 13: Potty Training Under Special Circumstances........................239

Chapter 14: Continuing the Potty Training 255

Chapter 15: Life Lessons Learned Through Potty Training Your Child 265

Introduction

My oldest daughter, Natalie, was about 18 months old when she started acting as if she was ready to use the potty, but I kept thinking she was too young to be potty trained. In addition, she was about to become a big sister to twins, and I was not sure I had the energy to attempt potty training at the time. When she was 22 months old, I put her in the thick training underwear, and I showed her how to sit on the potty chair. I would set a timer for ten minutes and make her sit on the potty chair every ten minutes until she went potty on it. Once she went potty for the first time, we celebrated by jumping around and cheering, we called her daddy at work so she could tell him, and we had a treat. From that

Natalie and the twins, Allison and Katelyn, when they were just a couple months old
PHOTO COURTESY OF MELANIE WILLIAMSON

point on, I asked her every 15 to 20 minutes if she had to go, and she was using the potty. I was thrilled, and I could not believe how easy that was. What I was not prepared for was the regression and subsequent rebellion.

Natalie was in training pants with few accidents around the house for almost a month when her twin sisters began rolling around, sitting up, and doing other things that demanded more of my attention. Up until this point, the twins had pretty much stayed in their playpens in our living room either sleeping or examining their baby toys. Natalie did not appreciate my decreased attention, to say the least.

She started having accidents around the house more often, or she would say she needed to go potty but only if I went with her. Once we were in the bathroom, she would insist I read her books or play with her. If I refused to stay in the bathroom and play with her, she would refuse to use the potty. Then, we got to the point where I would take her into the bathroom, she would refuse to use the potty, and then, she would run into the hallway and pee on the floor in the hallway. After three days of her not actually using the potty once, I could not handle it anymore, and I put her back in a diaper.

During the next 18 months, I tried every suggestion people gave me. I offered her rewards and treats, I let her go to the store and pick out her own underwear, I read her stories in the bathroom, and I even tried nothing for days in an effort to let her initiate using the potty again. Out of frustration,

I would get overly upset when she had accidents, and I would plead with her to use the bathroom. She was well older than 3 years old and still had regular accidents. I had to put her in a diaper every time we left the house because I could not trust her to tell me if she had to go. I also had to put her in a diaper whenever a babysitter came over because she absolutely refused to use the potty for a babysitter.

I was really starting to get worried she would not be potty trained in time to start preschool. All of my friends who had children the same general age as Natalie had potty trained their kids months earlier. Then, one day, she was potty trained. Natalie and I had been in a battle of wills for longer than a year, and she became potty trained only after she wanted to be potty trained. With all the mistakes and struggles I encountered with her, I was sincerely scared to potty train our twins.

Having done a lot more research and having talked to a lot more parents since then, I have been able to identify the many areas where I made mistakes with Natalie. First, I never really had a plan going into potty training; I just hoped she would figure it out if I kept taking her to the bathroom. I never worked with her on communicating to me when she needed to go. I was not at all prepared for her to regress, and last, but certainly not least, after she regressed, I started doing things out of desperation. My actions caused a great deal of confusion and inconsistency, which only encouraged Natalie to not be potty trained.

Reviewing my first potty training experience, I probably just as easily could write a book on how not to potty train a toddler. I would provide a breakdown of everything I did and encourage others not to do the same thing. In the hope that readers can learn to do it correctly the first time, however, this book will provide a detailed plan on how to quickly and effectively potty train a toddler.

Book Overview

This book covers a wide variety of issues related to potty training, as well as a step-by-step guide to get you through the potty training experience. To start, you will be provided with a history of potty training in the United States and how the process has changed over time. The age of potty training and the methods used have changed dramatically due to a number of factors, including the introduction of disposable diapers and the migration of mothers from the home to the workplace.

This book also will debunk common myths surrounding potty training and will consider the different factors of readiness for children. Once you understand how to tell if your child is ready for potty training, you will learn how to prepare for potty training. Chapter 5 through Chapter 9 will provide detailed information covering five of the most common potty training methods. This will provide you with the information you need to choose the method that is best for you and your child. Chapter 4 will go over some basic issues of bathroom etiquette, which a child must learn to be successfully potty trained.

The rest of the book will explain common problems, both medical and non-medical, that you might be confronted with while potty training. These issues include child reluctance, regression, constipation, and the fear of pooping. There is also a chapter dedicated to the topic of bed-wetting because it affects a great number of children and their parents. There will be information for parents of children with attention deficit disorder, attention deficit hyperactivity disorder, autism, and Down syndrome. Potty training multiples also will be addressed. The last chapter will offer advice in dealing with post-potty training issues, such as transitioning from the potty chair to the adult toilet, dealing with accidents or regression with older children, and knowing when it is OK to let your child go in a public restroom alone.

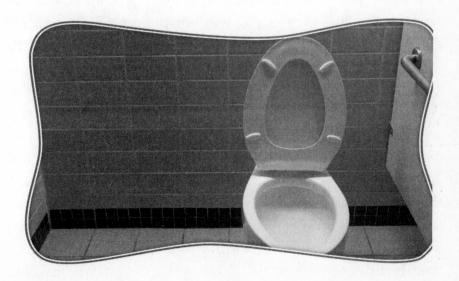

A note for parents and guardians of small children

Getting your child potty trained is an incredible step in parenting for both you and your child. As a parent, eliminating the need for diapers is tantamount to getting a raise in income, as there will be a dramatic decrease in expenses. A toddler should be changed six to eight times each day. That is equal to 2,190 to 2,920 diapers in a year. The average cost of Pampers® is 42 cents per diaper, which comes out to between $920 and $1,226 per year. You can reduce your diaper expense by using store-brand diapers, such as the up & up™ diapers sold at Target. Target brand diapers cost approximately 18 cents each. This means you will be spending $394 to $526 a year for diapers. Either way, potty training your child will save you hundreds, if not thousands, of dollars. In addition, these figures only represent the cost of diapers. Potty training means you also can stop spending money on diaper wipes and diaper rash cream. The cost of diaper wipes also varies greatly depending on the brand, but it is an expense you can eliminate with potty training. Although there are costs involved with the potty training process, they are minimal compared to the cost of diapers, and they are short term. After your child is potty trained, the only long-term expense you will have is the cost of underwear.

Getting your child potty trained also means independence from having to find a suitable place to change a child in public. Most parents have experienced the frustration of going to a public restroom only to find there is no changing table, or there is a changing table, but it is broken. Then, you are faced with the dilemma of finding a somewhat clean place to change your child. I am sure most parents have been in a situation where they have had to change their children in their vehicles, which typically is awkward.

Getting your child potty trained means no more last-minute runs to the store because you did not realize you only had one diaper left or being out in public when you realize you forgot the new package of wipes at home. Getting your child out of diapers also means no more diaper rash and no more need for diaper rash creams that are messy and do not wash off your hands easily. There are numerous benefits to potty training, which can be used as motivation to do it right from the beginning.

Potty training your children is more than teaching your child to use the potty. It is teaching your children how to identify the need to go to the bathroom, which will provide an increased awareness of their bodies. Potty training involves teaching your child how to flush the toilet and properly clean him or herself. Proper wiping is an important lesson that children do not always grasp right away, but it is essential to the prevention of infections. It is also about teaching your child the importance of privacy and modesty. Finally, potty training is about teaching your child the proper way to wash his or her hands and why hand washing is so important.

Advice from potty training veterans

One of the many things this book will provide is a selection of real parents sharing their experiences with potty training, dilemmas they faced, and how they got through it. Parents who were able to potty train their children at a younger than average age will share their experiences and advice. You also will read about parents who have had the opportunity to potty train both boys and girls and who will be able to discuss the differences between the two experiences. You will read stories from parents of multiples, the parents of a child with Asperger's syndrome, parents to children with attention deficit hyperactivity disorder (ADHD) and attention deficit disorder (ADD), as well as parents who faced some of the common potty training problems addressed throughout the book.

Reading about other parents' experiences will provide you with insight into the experience and the methods used. It also will offer you assurance during difficult times that your child is responding normally to the situation, and the problems you are facing are usual during the transition out of diapers. At times, potty training can be a frustrating experience, but it is important to stay focused on the end goal and to keep working with your child until that goal is accomplished. It is also helpful to have someone you can count on to call when you have had a less than successful day. Talking to another parent who has been through potty training will help diffuse any frustration you may feel and help you remain calm while with your toddler.

Common questions and difficulties with potty training

This book will answer many of the common questions parents have going into potty training, which often include questions about readiness and methods of training. Often, parents, such as myself, are faced with difficulties during the potty training process and are at a loss of what to do. This book will address these questions and provide insight to all the problems a parent might face. In addition, this book will address potty training issues specific to children with autism, ADHD, and ADD. The objective of this book is to provide all parents with the resources they need to potty train their toddlers.

Common myths about potty training

This book also will debunk many of the common myths surrounding potty training. These myths include believing your child is too young or not ready for potty training. There are several signs your child will demonstrate when he or she is physically and mentally ready to potty train, and these signs do not always coincide with a specific age. In addition, depending on the method of potty training you choose, children can be potty trained at a young age — often younger than 1 year old. Another common myth is that boys do not train as early or as quickly as girls do. Although potty training a boy can be more complicated, it does not need to be. Finally, many parents think potty training is going to be difficult, and they dread initiating the process. Each of these myths got started because it can be true. However, they are myths because the process and ease of potty training completely depends on the method you choose, your level of preparation, and your level of commitment once you begin the process. *Each of these myths will be covered in more detail in Chapter 1.*

Remember to stay positive

Potty training does not need to be as torturous as my first experience. It can be a rather simple and fun process if you are prepared. It is important to have a plan. It is also important to be prepared for roadblocks. Know ahead of time what you will do if your child refuses, regresses, or has issues using the potty. There are no new problems when it comes to potty training. Some parent somewhere has already faced anything you might experience during the process, and an answer to the problem can be found.

This book will provide you with an overview of commonly used potty training methods. These include the one-day training method, the child-temperament method, the no-cry method, the American Academy of Pediatrics recommended method, and the early training methods. For each method, you will be provided with the history and development of the method, as well as the research behind it. You also will be given step-by-step instructions on how to use the method, a list of needed supplies, and an explanation of the method's pros and cons.

As you will read in this book, there are many different approaches and theories regarding potty training, and many of them directly contradict each other. As with many parenting issues, many people have a clear opinion about potty training and how it should be done. Once you choose the potty training approach you are most comfortable with, stick to it. Do not let others convince you what you are doing is wrong or that you should do it their way instead.

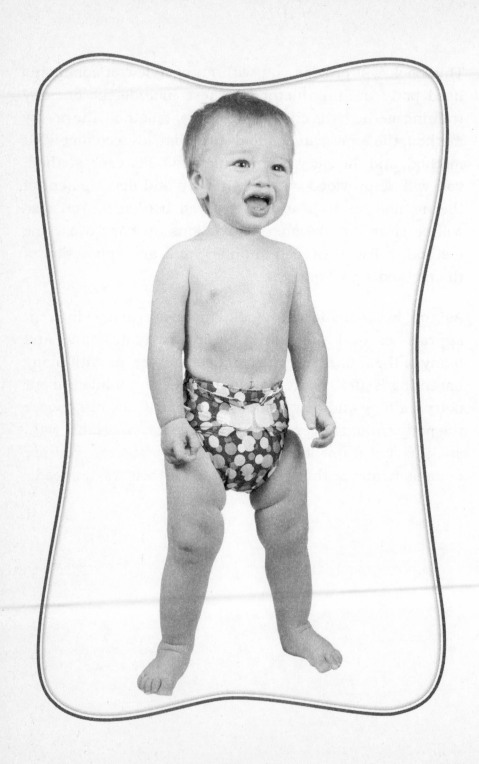

Chapter 1:
General Potty Training Facts

Understanding the general practice of potty training and why different methods are and are not used today will enable you to be even more prepared going into the process. This chapter includes a history of potty training in the United States, as well as common myths and statistical information. The history of potty training will give you insight into why things are so different now from how they were for early generations of potty training parents.

Understanding the common myths and why they are not true will give you the knowledge to know what advice is valid and what advice is not. Finally, understanding the statistical information on potty training will help you to know whether your child is at a normal stage of development or if there is cause to talk to your child's doctor.

Potty training is a process every parent must go through as his or her baby progresses through the toddler years. The act of potty training is teaching your child how to identify when he needs to pee or poop and then teaching him how to do that in a bathroom. In addition, potty training includes teaching your child how to clean himself properly, wash his hands, understand bathroom etiquette, and how to express his need to use the bathroom. The eventual goal is to have your child stop wearing diapers and be dependably dry and clean throughout the day. Potty training your toddler will free you from the ongoing expense of diapers and wipes, as well as the constant need to carry around a diaper bag and find restrooms with changing tables.

History of Potty Training

Often, older parents and grandparents will say they had their children potty trained by the time they were 18 months old or before they were 2. This might cause parents to feel discouraged about their child's lack of being potty trained. However, it is important to understand the drastic differences in potty training and diapers now compared to how they were before 1950.

Before the 1950s, parents used diapers made out of material. Most mothers throughout the 1800s and early 1900s used folded squares of linen or cotton flannel because it was convenient and absorbent. However, many frontier women were forced to use whatever was available to them. It was almost impossible to clean diapers in frontier life due to the lack of soap and other sanitizing agents, so most were rinsed and hung out to dry. Mothers were forced to wash diapers every day to ensure the baby always had clean diapers to wear. The process of changing and washing diapers was unending.

Due to the amount of mess and work involved in using cloth diapers at the time, mothers were highly motivated to potty train their children as early as possible. In addition to the mother's increased motivation, toddlers also were more motivated to get potty trained. Unlike disposable diapers of today that absorb wetness and leave babies feeling fresh and dry, cloth diapers were uncomfortable when wet or soiled. The constant discomfort made babies and young toddlers more willing to go along with potty usage.

In an effort to potty train, mothers would force their children to relieve themselves on a set schedule. Tactics to accomplish this would include forcing the child to sit on a potty or chamber pot until he peed or pooped or even using enemas and suppositories to force the child to poop at a specific time. After a period of training, the child would need to use the bathroom on a schedule, so the mother knew when to place him on the toilet. Although at first, it was simply a matter of timing, the child eventually would make the connection between sitting on the toilet and relieving himself. Once the connection was made, the child would be able to communicate the need to go pee or poop.

Mothers also used less drastic measures to potty train, which included learning their children's natural schedule and learning to observe how their children acted when needing to pee or poop. Children often have a signal, facial expression, or movement they do when they need to go to the bathroom. This signal can be observed when the child is only a few months old. The early potty training methods are based on learning to watch your child's signals. *They will be discussed further in Chapter 9 of this book.*

Potty training changed drastically in the late 1950s and early 1960s due to a variety of factors, including the introduction of the GE washing machine, which allowed users to control the temperature and speed of the machine. This relieved mothers of having to hand wash dirty cloth diapers every day. The disposable diaper also was invented in the late 1940s. Although still crude in their design, the disposable diapers were modified rapidly to be more effective, easier to use, and affordable. The disposable diaper was mass-marketed for the first time in 1948 by Johnson & Johnson. For a period, Johnson & Johnson controlled the disposable diaper market in the United States. Then in 1961, Procter & Gamble introduced Pampers.

In addition to these introductions, this period also saw the mass migration of mothers into the workplace. At the end of World War II, only 10 percent of women with children younger than 6 worked outside the home. However, by 1985, more than 50 percent of women with children younger than 6 worked outside the home. With the dramatic increase of women no longer staying home with their preschool-age children, the child-centered approach to potty training was introduced and quickly gained support. This approach emphasized the importance of not forcing a child to be potty trained at an early age. This approach worked well to accommodate mothers who had entered the workplace and could not be with their children all day.

Since this change in the overall approach to potty training, several different potty training methods have emerged that use a child-centered approach. Although child-centered methods vary in their expected duration, they all focus on not starting potty training until the toddler demonstrates the signs of readiness. *This will be discussed in Chapter 2.* In recent years, new methods have developed that focus on potty training children at younger ages. These methods argue that signs of readiness are either incorrect or highly subjective. They take a caring approach to parent-centered potty training, a stark contrast with the forceful methods of the previous generation that are now viewed as harsh and uncaring.

Child-Centered Approach Versus Parent-Centered Approach

The basic difference in potty training methods used today is whether they are parent-centered or child-centered. A parent-centered approach is one based on the parents making the decision to potty train their toddler before he demonstrates the signs of readiness. Although parent-centered approaches have proven successful, they are much more labor intensive for the parent. These methods require the parents to be around the child a majority of the time so they have the opportunity to watch the child's signs and to move him to the bathroom at appropriate times. A parent-centered approach is not ideal in households where both parents work unless there is an in-home child-care provider who understands what needs to be done and is dedicated to the process. Historically, the parent-centered approach has not been always the most caring approach, but with the research and early training methods available today, it can be accomplished in a caring manner.

A child-centered approach is one that depends upon waiting until the child demonstrates signs of readiness. It is referred to as child-centered because parents are expected to wait until the child shows a willingness and ability to use the bathroom. The child-centered approach discourages parents from forcing their children into potty schedules or taking their children out of diapers before the child is mentally and emotionally ready. Adopting the child-centered approach has resulted in the average age a child is potty trained to almost double since 1950. Potty training methods that use a child-centered approach instruct parents not even to consider potty training until after the child is 2 years old. This approach to potty training was strongly encouraged and endorsed by doctors such as Dr. T. Berry Brazelton, Dr. Benjamin Spock, and the American Academy of Pediatrics.

Important People in Potty Training History

Marion Donovan: Marion Donovan was a housewife in New York who was overwhelmed by the unending washing, bleaching, and air-drying of cloth diapers. In 1946, she cut up a plastic shower curtain, filled it with absorbent material, and then used snaps to hold it on her baby. After her baby had wet and soiled the absorbent material, she threw it in the trash. She called her creation a "boater." Although it took Donovan some time to find a store willing to carry her product, it was an immediate success with consumers, and she was eventually able to sell her company for $1 million.

Dr. T. Berry Brazelton: Dr. Brazelton is one of the pioneers of the child-centered approach. He first introduced the idea of child-centered potty training in the 1960s with his book, *A Child Orientated Approach to Toilet Training*. Dr. Brazelton believed forcing children to use the potty at a young age was leading to an increase in bathroom-related issues, such as bed-wetting, poop smearing, constipation, and withholding. Brazelton first introduced the idea of a child demonstrating he was ready for potty training and prepared a "signs of readiness" list for parents to look for in their children. He asserted that parents who potty trained their children before they showed signs of readiness were not really training their children. Instead, they were training themselves to force their children into the bathroom at the right times each day.

Dr. Brazleton later became a spokesperson for Pampers diapers and used his role as a doctor and spokesperson to encourage parents not to potty train their children at a young age. He also continued his research on potty training and today is seen as the creator of the child-centered approach and signs of readiness. Supporters of early potty training also hold Dr. Brazelton accountable for delayed potty training. Many early potty training supporters also have suggested that Dr. Brazleton encourages parents to hold off potty training because he is being paid to by Pampers, which clearly has a vested interest in how long children wear diapers.

Dr. Spock

Dr. Spock was one of the first pediatricians to study psychoanalysis and attempt to understand children's emotional and mental needs. In 1946, he published *Baby and Child Care*, which is still one of the best-selling books of all time. For generations, he was considered one of the top child-care professionals. He also came out publicly against the parent-centered approach to potty training. Dr. Spock encouraged parents to take a more relaxed approach to potty training and to potty train without force. He was opposed to the parent-centered methods that involved forcing the child to sit on the potty for long periods or making the child use the potty with the use of suppositories. He believed this approach had long-lasting negative affects on the children. Dr. Spock developed his own method of potty training that involved working with the child to potty train at his or her own pace.

Generally Accepted Basic Principles

Although there are many factors, such as minimum age and readiness, that are widely debated regarding potty training, a couple of key principles are accepted in all potty training methods. The first is that potty training should be a positive experience. It is important not to yell, criticize, or punish your toddler during potty training.  Doing these things will make the whole experience a negative one. It also can lead to your toddler to think there is something wrong with him or that pooping and peeing are somehow wrong. These feelings can cause children to try not to go, which can lead to medical problems as well as accidents. If you feel you are losing your temper during the potty training process, you need to take some time to yourself to regain your composure.

The second generally agreed upon principle is that you should not force your toddler to be potty trained. If, for any reason, your child is resisting, it is best to back off and talk to his doctor if you are concerned. Punishing your child, forcing him to sit in the bathroom for hours, or using enemas to force him to poop are not acceptable. These practices were used before the 1950s but have been proven wrong in the medical and psychological communities.

Regardless of the method you use, consistency is often the key to success, and these harsh tactics are not necessary to successfully potty train your toddler.

Potty Training Facts and Statistics

As previously discussed, potty training has changed drastically during the past few decades. Today, almost 95 percent of all parents in the United States use disposable diapers. The diaper industry is a multibillion-dollar industry, and diaper companies have expanded their markets into potty training. The introduction of disposable training pants has extended the average age of potty training even longer. In the last year, the diaper industry has pulled in $545 million in disposable training pants alone. Working parents do not have to worry about early potty training with the variety of sizes and styles available in disposable underpants. There are even disposable training pants available for school-age children.

These industry facts have initiated a minor movement back to early potty training. Some parents suggest that diaper companies are encouraging parents to extend potty training for making more money off the prolonged use of diapers, by using experts, such as Dr. Brazelton. However, that movement is still small due to the convenience of keeping a child in diapers. Despite the overall trend to wait until a toddler is older to potty train, early potty training advocates argue that the delay is not necessary.

CASE STUDY: POTTY
TRAINED OR HOUSEBROKEN?

Sue Giddings

I have three children, two boys and one girl. Although we had our ups and downs with each of the kids during potty training, I think the best story involves my oldest son. We had him housebroken before he was potty trained. We lived in Texas at the time, so it was warm year-round. We also had a nice fenced-in yard, and my husband stayed home with our son while I worked. We also had a small dog named Domino. Our son knew what it meant when people said "go potty." Every morning while my husband was getting the day started, he would open our back door, and call for Domino to go potty outside. Our son would follow her out. He often played outside, so we really did not think anything of him going outside with Domino. It took us a little while to realize that each morning when my husband told the dog to go outside, our son thought that was when he was suppose to go, too, so he was peeing first thing every morning outside with the dog. Once we realized this, we redirected him to the bathroom, but he was solidly housebroken before being potty trained.

The average age to potty train

On average, girls are potty trained by 29 months old, and boys are potty trained by 31 months old. However, these ages are the average; many children will be ready and willing to be potty trained well before these ages, and some might not be ready until much later. Ninety-eight percent of children are potty trained by 36 months. If your child is showing no signs of readiness by 36 months and all potty training attempts have failed, you might want to consult with the child's doctor. Although the reason for the lag in potty training might be perfectly normal and easy to deal with, you want to make sure there is not a larger medical problem preventing your child from being potty trained.

Typical potty training duration

The amount of time it takes a parent to potty train his or her toddler depends primarily on the potty training method. Although there are methods available that, when strictly followed, can have your child potty trained in a day, the majority of parents take three to six months to potty train their child. To say a toddler is potty trained is to say the child is reliably dry and mess free throughout the day, including while in public and away from the house, and the child can adequately communicate the need to use the potty. Although typically saying a child is potty trained means the child initiates the need to go to the bathroom, some children may need reminding periodically throughout the day to use the potty. This does not mean the child is not properly or fully potty trained. Some children get distracted easily and wait until the very last second to use the potty, which can sometimes lead to accidents. Referring to a child as potty trained does not necessarily refer to whether the child wets the bed. Bed-wetting is a separate condition. *Chapter 11 will discuss this in detail.*

Physiological facts about boys' and girls' digestive systems

When a child eats, food travels to the small intestines, where the nutrients are taken out of the food and absorbed into the bloodstream. This process can take up to four hours after eating. The food is then passed to the large intestines, where it turns into poop and builds up until the child feels the need to poop. Based on your child's eating schedule, it is likely he will need to poop at roughly the same times each day. Learning your child's pooping schedule will help greatly during potty training. Parents often report that their child resisted pooping in the potty far more than peeing in the potty. Knowing when your child typically needs to poop can allow you to suggest he sit in the bathroom with you or take a quick potty break.

Becoming aware of your child's pooping schedule also will let you know how many times a day your child normally poops. This information is good for two reasons. First, it will let you know when you should suggest he go sit on the potty. Second, it will help you become aware of problems quickly. Both diarrhea and constipation are common problems, and the quicker you realize your child has either diarrhea or constipation, the quicker you can help him. How many times a child should poop each day is unique to the child. Although once a day might be normal for some children, three times a day might be normal for others. Do not worry about how often your child poops unless it changes drastically, or there are other related issues, such as frequent cramping and painful gas. In addition, if your child poops less than three times over the course of a week, it may be a sign of constipation. *These medical conditions will be discussed in Chapter 12.*

Boys: sit or stand?

Although boys eventually will need to learn to pee standing up, when they are first being potty trained, it is important to teach them to pee sitting down. There are several reasons for this. First, in order to pee and poop, a toddler needs to be able to relax his muscles. As your child gets older, he will learn how to relax his muscles separately, which will allow him to only pee or only poop. However, as a toddler, he might not be able to stop himself from pooping while he pees or from peeing while he poops. If you potty train him to pee standing up, this might lead to him accidentally pooping on the floor while he pees.

The second reason boys should be potty trained sitting down is because, as toddlers, they will not have learned fully how to ensure their pee only goes in the toilet. Teaching him to use the potty sitting down will ensure he does not accidentally pee on himself while standing. This can cause your son to feel embarrassed and may derail your potty training efforts temporarily. Once your son is consistently staying dry during the day, you can introduce him to the idea of standing while he pees.

Finally, the third reason you should potty train boys sitting down is potential height issues. Although at home you might have a potty chair or stool that will ensure he is tall enough to pee in the toilet while standing, you will not have that guarantee in public. There might be instances where public urinals are not low enough for your son to stand comfortably. If your son is newly potty trained or strong-willed, he might refuse to pee sitting down, which can lead to an accident. It will be easier to have a boy pee standing when he is used to sitting down than to have a boy pee sitting down when he is used to standing up. *Teaching boys how to pee standing up will be covered in Chapter 14.*

Overcoming Myths about Potty Training

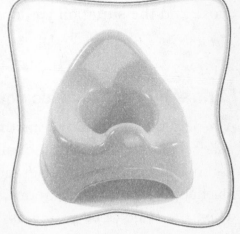

Potty training is one of many topics parents frequently talk about with other parents. Although seeking out other parents' advice often is helpful, there are two negative consequences of this. The first is being scared by horror stories.

There often will be parents who want to share their horrific potty training story to parents just starting to think about potty training. However, it is important to remember that every child is different, and every child will respond differently to potty training. Just because your neighbor's son took 18 months to potty train does not mean you will have similar difficulties.

The second negative consequence is the perpetuation of potty training myths. Just because other parents might say something as if it were fact does not mean it is true for your child. For example, in most cases, it takes longer to potty train boys than girls. However, that does not mean boys should not be potty trained until they are older. If a young boy is showing interest in the potty and signs of readiness, he should be introduced to potty training. Do not ignore the signs of readiness because someone told you to wait or that your child is too young. Another common myth is that once you start potty training, you cannot go back to diapers. Once again, whether or not you end up putting your child back into diapers depends on the method you chose and the situation you are dealing with.

Myth #1: My child is too young

A variety of early training methods focus on potty training children before the traditional signs of readiness. These parent-centered approaches are safe and caring, as well as effective in many situations. These methods might start when the child is as young as 3 months old. Before 1950, the majority of children were potty trained by the time they were 18 months old. Early potty training methods are time intensive, and they do not work for everyone, which is OK. However, it can be done, and it does not matter how young your child is.

It is important to not put too much emphasis on your child's age when determining his readiness for potty training. If your child is 18 months old and is showing all the signs of readiness, you might want to consider initiating potty training. Taking a parent-centered approach might lead you to potty training your child at the earliest possible convenience. What is most important is waiting until you are ready to fully commit to potty training. Regardless of how old your child is, you need to be prepared to take the time to potty train and to deal with accidents if and when they happen.

Myth #2: Potty training is not easy

As mentioned earlier in this chapter, the majority of parents take three to six months to potty train their toddler, and during this time, parents likely will deal with several accidents. Books and articles on potty training often spend a great deal of time discussing how to deal with reluctant or resistant children. This information often can lead parents to see potty training as a hurdle they need to overcome. In addition, hearing stories of difficulties from other parents can intimidate parents preparing to potty train their child.

Although many parents are apprehensive going into the potty training process, it does not have to be a difficult process. The more prepared you are before initiating potty training with your toddler, the easier it will be. It is important always to stay positive and encouraging with your child. If your child is having fun during the potty training process, he will be more willing to cooperate. You can prepare your child in a wide variety of ways to ensure an easy transition, which will be discussed throughout this book. If your child is particularly resistant to potty training, you can look into the no-cry methods of potty training, which include Dr. Spock's method. *These will be discussed further in Chapter 8.*

Myth #3: My child is not ready yet

It might be difficult for a parent to know for sure if his child is ready to be potty trained. Earlier in this chapter, we discussed the average age of boys and girls when they are potty trained. This general information is provided to give parents a big-picture view of potty training in the United States. Do not use the average age of potty training as a guideline when determining your own child's readiness. Determining the right time to potty train is something you need to trust your instincts on. No one knows your child better than you do. Do not let others tell you when you should or should not potty train your child.

Look for signs in your toddler when deciding if he is ready for potty training. *This will be discussed further in Chapter*

2. Avoid waiting for a certain age, and avoid letting others tell you whether your child is ready. Children do not all potty train at the same age, and they do not all potty train at the same speed. Only you, as the parent, can make that determination. Being ready might mean different things to different people. In addition, if you are ready to commit to potty training, your child will likely adjust. When reading over the signs of readiness in Chapter 2, it is also important to keep in mind that not all children display all the signs of readiness. You should not wait until your child demonstrates each sign.

Myth #4: Making a child wear wet or dirty underpants will encourage fewer accidents

Some parents think making a child wear wet or dirty underpants will "teach them a lesson" and reduce accidents. However, this actually might have the opposite effect. The child will grow accustomed to the smell and feel of wet or dirty underpants. It will desensitize him and actually increase accidents because he will not mind being dirty or wet. Unless you immediately changed his diaper every time he pooped before, he likely is already accustomed to the smell of his own poop. Forcing your child to wear wet or soiled underpants can lead to urinary tract infections, vulvovaginitis, and diaper rash. It is always best to change your child as soon as you realize there was an accident.

However, knowing your child's temperament also will help in this situation. *Chapter 7 describes the most common child temperaments and how knowing your child's temperament can aid in potty training.* Children who are sensory-orientated do not like to be wet or messy. These children likely cried every time they had a dirty diaper as a baby and asked to be changed as soon as they learned how to communicate that need verbally. Sensory-orientated children will be motivated by the desire to stay clean and dry. Although you should still change your toddler as soon as an accident occurs, the act of having an accident can help motivate sensory-orientated children to pee and poop in the potty.

Myth #5: Tough discipline is the key to potty training

All modern methods of potty training, including child-centered and parent-centered approaches, discourage using discipline during the potty training process. All modern sources agree that tough discipline does not encourage potty training, and it actually can hinder potty training because it confuses and upsets the child. Your child may think you are mad at him for peeing and pooping, as opposed to the accident. This may lead to your child withholding in order to avoid punishment, and withholding can lead to serious medical problems.

When a child repeatedly has accidents, a parent might feel he is doing it on purpose. However, it is important to remember that potty training is a process, sometimes a long process. Children who get distracted easily or who are active might be more inclined to have accidents. Punishing your child will not discourage accidents because he is not having them intentionally. What a punishment will do is make the potty training experience a negative one filled with frustration for both you and your child. Find a way to deal with your own frustrations without taking it out on your toddler or even letting him know you are frustrated.

Myth #6: Your child's life will be ruined if you do not potty train correctly

Some researchers, such as Sigmund Freud, have put so much emphasize on the repercussions of potty training that some parents might feel they are permanently damaging their child's emotional well-being, confidence, or self-image during potty training. However, this is not likely the case. What is important to protecting your child's mental and emotional well-being is remaining calm and relaxed. Avoid getting so stressed that you start stressing out your child. This will hinder the potty training efforts and make the whole situation frustrating for everyone.

Current research does not show a connection between potty training and later psychological problems. However, ineffective potty training can cause a delay in entry to preschool, and some researchers believe it leads to bathroom problems, such as constipation and withholding, in school-age children. In addition, research has shown that the later a parent waits to initiate potty training, the longer the potty training process takes.

Myth #7: It is best to potty train during the summer

Potty training during summer months means your child likely will be wearing less clothing, which means less for you to wash when there is an accident. It also means you can spend more time outside, so accidents do not happen on a carpeted floor. However, this has no influence on how quickly or easily your child potty trains. It just means you will have less to clean up. If you do choose to potty train over the summer, keep in mind that children are less likely to announce they have to use the potty if they do not want to stop playing and go in the house. You will need to push potty breaks.

If you have older children, trying to potty train during the summer months might be more difficult. If your older children are involved in a variety of daily activities, it might be difficult to allow your toddler enough free time at home to spend potty training. Although school-age children are likely busy during the school year, their activities will be limited to evenings and weekends.

The only time of year that you should avoid potty training is over the winter holidays. Thanksgiving and Christmas often are filled with large family visits and traveling. These can lead to increased accidents because your toddler may not always be made aware of where the bathroom is in enough time to avoid an accident, or he is so distracted by visiting family that he forgets to go.

Myth #8: Accidents are a sign your child was not ready for potty training

Whether you are adopting the one-day potty party approach or one of the slower no-cry approaches to potty training, each approach instructs parents to be prepared for accidents. Accidents are an acceptable part of potty training, and there is no set limit to how many accidents a child should or should not have. It is more important to observe whether a child appears to understand the process or if he seems confused when you are discussing the potty. Each time your child has an accident; you should remind him that pee and poop belong in the toilet.

As already mentioned, children potty train at different speeds. If your child is having multiple accidents, that does not automatically mean he was not ready to be potty trained. It might just mean you need to adjust your approach. Rely less on him announcing when he needs to go and rely more on planned bathroom breaks. If you feel your child is resisting, you might need to take a break from potty training. *Suggestions for dealing with a reluctant or resistant child will be discussed throughout the book and will be the focus of Chapter 10.*

Myth #9: Once you take your child out of diapers, you can never go back

Some parents hold the firm belief that once you take a child out of diapers, going back will only confuse the situation and derail the potty training process. Likewise, some potty training methods advocate this approach. However, there are some potty training methods that support continued diaper use throughout potty training. In addition, situations may arise that warrant you halting potty training and allowing your child to go back to diapers for a time.

Putting a diaper on your child after you have introduced potty training will not ruin your efforts completely. If your child is not responding well to potty training and urgently resisting your efforts, putting him back into diapers and backing off for a time may be exactly what he needs to adjust to the idea of the transition. Allowing your child to continue wearing diapers at night, while traveling long distances, or while sick will help avoid accidents that can sincerely upset and discourage your toddler.

Chapter 2:
Ready or Not

When deciding on the right time to potty train your child, you need to consider a few things. First on the list is which potty training method to use. All methods can be divided into two basic categories: early potty training and child-centered potty training. Early potty training means potty training before your child is 2 years old. Child-centered potty training refers to potty training methods that rely on your child demonstrating the signs of readiness. These are the signs that have been accepted and promoted by the American Academy of Pediatrics. If following these signs of readiness, most children are not ready for potty training until after the age of 2. However, early potty training methods instruct parents to look for other signs of readiness, which typically are demonstrated at a younger age. Regardless of the potty training method you choose, you will need to be aware of what signs you should be looking for in your children.

Is There a Readiness Factor?

Although history has shown that children are capable of being potty trained at a fairly young age, many professionals and proponents of the child-centered approach argue that potty training children before they are fully ready can lead to a number of bathroom issues, including constipation and withholding. When a child refuses to pee when she needs to she is withholding. Proponents have argued that potty training children before they are ready can cause lasting psychological damage. This presumed damage is derived from the child's lack of control over the situation, as well as their view of their body and bodily functions. This was a popular belief throughout the 1960s and 1970s, and child-care professionals such as Dr. Brazelton and Dr. Spock promoted it. This belief and encouragement toward the child-centered approach also has been strongly advocated by the diaper industry, primarily Johnson & Johnson and Procter & Gamble. However, later research has shown that early potty training, in and of itself, does not cause psychological damage.

Addressing both sides of the argument

As with any argument, there are two sides to the readiness debate. These professionals argue there is no significant evidence that supports the benefits of waiting until children demonstrate the prescribed readiness factors. Many who support early potty training argue that Brazelton's campaign to persuade parents to prolong potty training was primarily a tactic to keep children in diapers. This argument is supported by the fact that Brazelton has worked as a consultant for Procter & Gamble to endorse Pampers diapers. Brazelton even appears in Pampers commercials and encourages parents to let their children stay in diapers as long as the children want to. One of Brazelton's famous quotes is, "Don't rush your toddler into toilet training or let anyone else tell you it's time. It's got to be his choice."

John Rosemond feels Brazelton's position is unfounded. Rosemond is a family psychologist who strongly advocates early potty training. His position is based on his personal research, as well as other current research on early potty training. Rosemond personally has written a great deal to promote early potty training and instruct parents on how to potty train early. He was quoted as saying it is a "slap to the intelligence of a human being that one would allow a baby to continue soiling and wetting himself past age 2." Brazelton has responded to Rosemond's position by saying, "Parents are feeling very guilty, and people like Rosemond are making them feel more guilty, not less… and the child's only recourse is to withhold urine and stool in protest." Brazelton believes the increase is caused by parents pushing their children out of diapers before they are ready. Rosemond argues the increase in problems is caused by parents not potty training their children early enough.

Potty training younger than 2

Early potty training typically is defined as potty training a child younger than 2 years of age. The signs of readiness for early potty training are vastly different from the signs for later potty training, and the signs vary depending on how young your child is. For example, infant potty training, which is potty training children between the ages of birth to 6 months old, bases readiness on age, as opposed to actual signs. This form of potty training is often referred to as elimination, and it is the method commonly used in tribal cultures where disposable, or even cloth diapers, typically are unavailable. The method is reminiscent of Pavlov's dog experiment in which he got the dogs to salivate when they heard the sound of a bell. Essentially, infant potty training is teaching infants to respond to an auditory cue by voiding. The advantage of infant potty training is that your child is essentially potty trained by the time she reaches her toddler years. In addition, the child never or rarely wears diapers, which drastically decreases cost. The disadvantages of infant potty training include the time commitment needed and the constant need to clean up after your child during the process.

Children older than 6 months can be potty trained in a similar fashion, which drastically will decrease diaper usage and save money. The disadvantage of early potty training is that it can take several months to accomplish, and during that time, your toddler will have frequent accidents. Despite this, the potty training process will be completed by the time your toddler is 2 years old. Early potty training can be started as soon as the parents are ready, regardless of the child's age or the child's ability to demonstrate the AAP's recommended signs of readiness.

Potty training when the child seems ready (2 to 4 years)

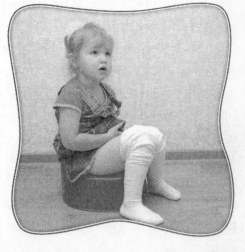

There are three basic areas of readiness: physical or physiological, cognitive, and emotional. To say a toddler is physically ready to be potty trained means the child can hold her pee or poop until she gets to a bathroom, she can walk to the bathroom on her own, and she can dress and undress herself. For a toddler to be mentally ready, she needs to be able to understand simple directions and follow them. Being able to follow simple instructions means the child can do more than one thing. For example, you can say to your child, "Go in the bathroom, and pull your pants down." These are two distinct instructions for your toddler to understand and follow. She also needs to be able to communicate at a basic level. Finally, to be emotionally ready, she needs to be willing to transition out of diapers and be prepared to deal with the change.

The following list provides the signs of readiness that the American Academy of Pediatrics asserts are necessary for potty training.

- ☆ The child can stay dry for at least two hours at a time.
- ☆ The child is dry after naps.
- ☆ The child has regular bowel movements.
- ☆ Either through words or actions, the child can let others know she is about to pee or poop.
- ☆ The child can follow simple instructions.
- ☆ The child can walk independently.
- ☆ The child likes to be clean and will request her diaper to be changed after she has pooped.
- ☆ The child will ask to use the potty.
- ☆ The child will ask to wear big-kid underpants.

The following tables show the different areas of development and the approximate age at which children develop different abilities. These tables show that the abilities needed for potty training typically are present at about 24 months of age.

TABLE 1: Physiological and Motor Skill Development

Ability	Age
Aware of the need to pee or poop	12–18 months
Learns to walk	18–24 months
Ability to control muscles to hold in poop	18–24 months
Increased ability to sit still	18–24 months
Able to help dress and undress herself	24–36 months
Maturing of digestive system needed to decrease or eliminate bed-wetting	3 years +

Source: American Academy of Pediatrics

TABLE 2: Cognitive and Verbal Development

Ability	Age
Starts to see connection between cause and effect	0–12 months
Starts to associate the feeling of a full bladder with peeing	12–18 months
Starts to talk	18–24 months
Ability to act toward a goal	18–24 months
Increased understanding of verbal instruction	18–24 months
Increased ability to remember routines	24–36 months
Ability to role play	24–36 months
Ability to stop an activity to go to the bathroom without being prompted	3 years +

Source: American Academy of Pediatrics

TABLE 3: Emotional and Social Development

Ability	Age
Enjoys praise	0–12 months
Ability to mimic others	12–18 months
Wants to do things independently	18–24 months
Starts working toward mastery in interests	18–24 months

Desire to gain approval from parents	18-24 months
Gets pleasure in learning new things	24-36 months
Starts to become aware of gender differences	24-36 months
Enjoys earning simple rewards; can be encouraged through the use of sticker charts	3 years +

Source: American Academy of Pediatrics

The fewer signs of readiness your child demonstrates, the more you will need to do for her during potty training and once she is potty trained. For example, if your child physically is not able to pull up her own pants, then you will need to do that for her each time she uses the bathroom. Potty training methods based on the signs of readiness argue that children who are not demonstrating most of the signs of readiness will have a difficult time being potty trained or potty training attempts will fail until the child is older and more developed.

Knowing When to Start

Regardless of the potty training method you choose, there are times you should not attempt to potty train your child. Children do not always adjust well to changes in routine and schedule. Unexpected changes can cause any child to have increased accidents or completely refuse to use the potty. For this reason, it is important not to attempt potty training immediately before or after a dramatic change in the child's daily life. Dramatic changes might include moving, a new baby joining the family, or a change in the family unit, such as a divorce or parental separation.

Although some changes cannot be anticipated, such as a sudden death or a move caused by an unexpected disaster, it is important to be aware of any upheaval your child might feel. Remember that when and where your toddler pees and poops is something she controls. If there are sudden changes in her life, she may want to regain control by refusing to pee and poop where you want her, too.

Identifying your child's desire to use the potty

Not all children will demonstrate a desire to use the potty. If your toddler does show an interest in using the potty, it is important to allow her to explore that interest. Even if you do not believe your toddler is ready to start potty training, talking about using the potty and letting her into the bathroom at this point will help encourage natural interest. If you have decided to wait until your child demonstrates the AAP-recommended signs of readiness, wait until your child is at least 2 years old. The majority of the readiness signs will not be present before the age of 2. If you are choosing an early potty training method, you will be incorporating your child's natural interest into the potty training process. Depending on how early you start potty training, your child might already have experience using the potty. This experience can come from you allowing your child to sit on the toilet or potty chair or flush the toilet. In addition, your child might have a higher understanding of what to do if you have allowed her to observe you using the potty, watch potty training videos, or read potty storybooks.

The Parents' Influence

Parents make all the difference in the world when it comes to potty training. This point will be emphasized repeatedly throughout this book. Potty training is an opportunity for you to shower your child with love and praise. You will be walking your child through a major accomplishment in life, and it is important to always keep that in mind. Potty training is an enormous transition for toddlers, and toddlers need their parents to understand that fact. Whether potty training will be a positive experience or a negative experience will be depend on your influence. If you make it fun and stress-free, then your toddler will have fun and feel stress-free. Likewise, if you are frustrated and anxious throughout the entire process, your toddler will be, too.

The importance of commitment

It is important that all caregivers involved with the child are equally committed. This means parents, babysitters, day-care workers, and any other friends or family members who are with the child for any period. It will be counterproductive if you are working with your child all weekend and then Monday morning, the babysitter puts your child in diapers instead of encouraging her to use the potty. This is especially important if your child is with a caregiver the majority of the day. The caregiver will need to be equally positive and excited about the potty training experience.

Until the child is reliably dry all day, she will need regular reminders to use the bathroom and likely will need assistance or supervision. You will need to make sure everyone is on the same page. Explain your chosen method of potty training to each of your child's caregivers and what they need to do while with your child. Give your child's caregivers an opportunity to ask questions if they need to.

Some day-care centers are not always willing to work with parents when it comes to potty training. They want the children in their care to either be in diapers or be completely potty trained. It is understandable; they are caring for multiple children, and they do no want to deal with accidents in the general and play areas. However, if the day-care center is not willing to work with you, you might want to consider a different child-care situation during this crucial time.

The importance of communication

Communication is important in all areas. You and your partner need to communicate with each other regarding the method of potty training you plan to use. You need to communicate clearly with your child-care providers, and you need to communicate clearly with your child during potty training. Once you are ready to present potty training to your child, everyone involved needs to be completely clear about what needs to be done. Inconsistency or changing methods halfway through potty training likely will confuse the child.

Your child needs to fully understand what is going on during the potty training process, what you want her to do, and how she needs to do it. Potty training is not just about getting a child to go pee and poop in the potty. It is also about teaching the child to identify when she needs to go, how she needs to clean herself after going, how to flush the toilet, and how to wash her hands when done. Often, children want to know what exactly is going on and may ask questions regarding what exactly pee and poop is and where it came from. This level of curiosity is natural and may help the potty training process. Show your child a diagram of the digestive system and explain what happens to the food she eats.

The importance of organization and order

In all areas of life, children thrive on order. Predictability and routine help children feel secure and adjust to transitions well. Potty training is a major change for a child, and the process needs to be as organized and seamless as possible. Otherwise, your child might resist the process, and that will make potty training much more difficult. You cannot force a child to use the potty, and you want to avoid inciting a battle of wills. To keep things organized, make sure everything you need is ready before starting the potty training process. Throughout potty training, make sure everything your child needs is well stocked. Do not attempt potty training right before a big trip or holiday. Doing so might sabotage your efforts.

Parental Readiness

As important as it is for your child to be ready for potty training, you as the parent also must have a healthy attitude and realistic expectations before starting this experience. The first step to preparing yourself for potty training is identifying how you really think and feel about it. What are your goals, and are they realistic? The following list of questions will help you identify your goals, motivations, and concerns about potty training:

- ☆ Why do I want my child potty trained now?
- ☆ Do I have a deadline to potty train my child?
- ☆ Do I feel it is essential that my child be potty trained though the night? Why?
- ☆ What would I do if my child had an accident while we were in public?
- ☆ What would I do if my child had an accident while we had company over at the house?
- ☆ How would I respond if I found my child playing with poop?

☆ How would I feel if my child started talking about her poop in front of other people?

☆ How long would my child have to be potty trained before I would take her out in public without a diaper on?

☆ How fast do I expect my child to potty train?

☆ How will I feel if it takes longer than expected?

☆ What is my biggest concern about potty training?

☆ Do I feel pressure from other parents to potty train my child?

Answering these questions will help you determine how you feel about potty training, and these questions will help you identify areas where you need to work preparing yourself before potty training your child. For example, if thinking about how you would react to your child having an accident in public causes feelings of overwhelming embarrassment, you need to prepare a plan of action. Decide now what you will do if that happens. These questions also will help you determine exactly why you are considering potty training now. If the reason is that you feel both you and your toddler are ready to make the transition, you are mentally in the right place. If you are doing it because your best friend's daughter is now potty trained and she is two months younger than your daughter, you should probably wait.

Mental preparation can be the hardest to achieve. If you go into potty training believing it will fail, your toddler will understand your negative emotions and not be motivated to potty train. Children have an innate ability to read their parents' feelings. It is vitally important to the process for all parents and guardians to go into potty training excited and optimistic. Parents actually should be overly excited because toddlers respond well to excitement and enthusiasm. If parents introduce potty training as if it is the best thing in the world and more fun than toys, their toddler will embrace that level of enthusiasm.

For this reason, it is also important not to associate negative words with using the potty, such as referring to poop as "stinky" or "gross." You want your child to be excited to poop. Be prepared to celebrate it and congratulate your child for making it. It is important to get over any embarrassment you feel talking about bathroom activities. Keep in mind that you have been dealing with your child's pee and poop since the day she was born. Choose potty terms you will be most comfortable using. For example, it is OK if you are more comfortable using the word "bottom" than "butt."

If you are still embarrassed talking about pee and poop, then practice with your partner. Say the words aloud, and say them repeatedly. In addition, practice answering questions you might find embarrassing or uncomfortable. For example, a little boy might ask his mommy if she has a pee-pee also, or a little girl might ask her daddy why he pees standing up. Be prepared to answer these types of questions with short, simple, and honest answers. For example, a mother can tell her

son that she does not have a pee-pee like him because she is a girl, and boys and girls are different. Although you can also teach your toddler when and where it is appropriate to talk about the potty, you need to feel comfortable talking about it with your toddler.

CASE STUDY: CHOOSING A TIME THAT IS BEST FOR EVERYONE

Gerry Harkins

When my oldest three children were in diapers, we were still using cloth diapers. Potty training was easy, I think, because the cloth diapers were very uncomfortable when they were wet or soiled. Toddlers did not want to wear wet and soiled diapers any more than parents wanted to wash them. It was common for children to be potty trained by two years old. We just showed them where the potty was, praised them when they went, and then put them in regular underwear. Diapers today are so absorbent, children do not even know when they are wet. It is not uncomfortable for them to pee and poop in their pants. Likewise, parents do not need to wash those soiled diapers every day, so there is no big rush to get the kids potty trained.

When my youngest was potty trained, things went a little differently. My mother lived with us at the time, and she had Alzheimer's disease. Although she was wonderful and loving to my youngest, she was not always kind to my second youngest, who was five years old at the time. My mother's doctor told me that she was so kind to my youngest because she saw her clearly as a baby, but once she was potty trained, my mother likely would be unkind to her as well. Because of this, I kept my youngest in diapers until I could find a good place for my mother to live, where they were familiar with her disease. This took a little time, and my youngest was well over three by the time my mother moved out. Ironically, my little girl already knew what to do. She lived in a house with two parents, a grandmother, and four older siblings. Being around so many people all the time made her clearly aware of when people went into the bathroom and what they did in there. When my mother moved out, we took my youngest out of diapers, and she started using the potty right away.

Logistics

To be logistically prepared, you need to make sure the potty seat or potty chair is easily accessible. Make sure the bathroom is stocked with toilet paper, and it is easily reachable. Your toddler also will need a stool to reach the sink, and you will need to make sure there is plenty of hand soap and extra towels nearby. Everything your toddler needs to use the potty successfully should be within her grasp. This can be accomplished over a period of time. Do not feel you need to prepare fully for potty training in a day.

Let your child start spending more time in the bathroom before potty training. This might make you aware of a logistical need you did not think of earlier. For example, you might realize the toilet paper dispenser is not within reach for your toddler. You may also realize there is nowhere to keep the potty storybooks. Realizing logistical difficulties before initiating potty training will enable you to fix them and be better prepared. *Chapter 3 further discusses the items you might need to purchase before potty training.*

Unified front and expectations between parents

In order to avoid confusion and inconsistency, it is important that all caregivers, especially the parents of the toddler, are in agreement regarding the timing and method of potty training. This extends to parents who might not live together, grandparents, babysitters, and other child-care providers. Creating a unified front will help your child get through the potty training process faster. It also will show your toddler that everyone is cooperating and working together. These are important lessons for your toddler to learn, and she will learn them by observing the behavior of caregivers.

However, there are situations in which creating absolute consistency is not an option; for example, if your child is in a day-care facility that is unable to accommodate special requests regarding potty training, or if your relationship with the child's other parent is not a positive one and that person is unwilling to work with you. In these situations, it might be useful to explain "home rules." Toddlers understand that there are rules they need to follow. If the bathroom procedures are different at home than they are at other places where your child spends time, explain to your child that there are home rules. While your child is at home, she will follow the home rules for the bathroom, and when your child is somewhere else, she will need to follow the rules there. This is obviously not the ideal situation, but it might be the only solution in a difficult situation.

"Home rules" also can be applied to going to the bathroom at home and going to the bathroom in public. For example, at home it might be OK for your child to go in the potty by herself. However, while in public, it is important for her to understand she cannot run off to the potty without you. You also can make asking potty-related questions or discussing potty activities a home rule. This will help teach your child when and where it is appropriate to talk about the potty. Finally, leaving the bathroom door open might be a home rule. Allowing your child to leave the door open will allow you to easily check on her and allow her to call for help easily if needed.

Chapter 3:
The Preparation

Preparation can make a significant difference during the potty training process. Parents and children who are prepared for potty training will have a better understanding of what needs to be done before the actual potty training. This likely will expedite the whole process. Although potty training still can be derailed by a number of events, preparation is also a good thing and will never hurt the process. Being prepared is an important key to success in any situation, and demonstrating this to your toddler at a young age will help him as he grows.

Make it Obvious

It is important to make the bathroom and potty chair as easy to find and accessible to your toddler as possible. This might mean removing baby gates or leaving the bathroom door open. Until your toddler can remember where the bathroom is, walk with him or point him in the right direction. Put the potty chair in the bathroom weeks before initiating potty training. Then each time you go potty, take your toddler with you, and tell him what the chair is for. You also can hang a mirror on the wall directly across from the potty chair. Toddlers typically love looking in mirrors, and it will encourage him to sit on the chair.

You also can cut out pieces of construction paper in the shape of little feet and tape them to the floor leading from the living room to the bathroom. Although your toddler probably already knows where the bathroom is located, the feet will be a fun reminder. Another way to make it obvious is by decorating the door to the bathroom or by placing a sign on the bathroom door. Anything you can do to get your toddler more involved and draw more attention to the bathroom will be helpful during potty training.

Place the potty in the an obvious place

If you are planning to use a potty chair and not a potty seat (which will be explained in further detail later in this chapter), obviously, the ideal place to keep the potty chair is in the bathroom. Keeping the potty chair in the bathroom will get your son used to the idea that the bathroom is where he needs to go when he is ready to use the toilet. Keeping the potty chair in the bathroom also will make it easier to dump the potty chair and clean it between uses.

However, keeping the potty chair in the bathroom might not be ideal for the setup in your house. For example, many older homes only have bathrooms on the second floor, while the living areas are on the first floor. A child just learning to use the bathroom likely will not make it all the way upstairs in time to use the bathroom successfully. If you decide not to keep your potty chair in the bathroom, do not move it around. Choose a spot for the chair, and leave it there. This will prevent an accident if your toddler tries to find and use the potty without telling you first. If you need to take the potty chair to a different room or area to empty it or clean it, bring it back to its original location as soon as possible.

The second best place to put a potty chair is in the kitchen. Again, kitchen floors are typically hard surfaces, such as linoleum or tile, which will make cleanup easier in case of an accident. In addition, kitchens are generally centrally located on the first floor and easy to get to from the living room. Finally, as a parent, you likely spend a good deal of time in the kitchen, so you will be able to continue potty training while maintaining your normal daily chores and activities.

It is not a good idea to put the potty chair in an area where the child could sit on the potty chair and watch the television at the same time. Although this might seem ideal if your child does not want to sit on the potty chair, it will create an unneeded distraction. If your child is watching television, he either will not go because he is too distracted, or he will go without realizing what he is doing because he is too distracted. Finally, if you let your child sit on the potty chair to watch television, the potty chair will become a piece of furniture in his mind. It is important that the child is always aware of what the potty chair is there for and what he should be doing while sitting on the potty chair.

Celebrate when you use the potty

Although this might sound foolish or embarrassing, it is important for your toddler to know everyone in the family uses the toilet. After using the bathroom, happily tell your child you went pee or poop in the potty. Use the new bathroom vocabulary words (discussed in the next section) that you and your partner decide on. When other family members use the bathroom, encourage them to tell your toddler about it. Remind your toddler each time that big people do not wear diapers, and they go pee and poop in the potty. This consistent reinforcement will not only help prepare your toddler for potty training, but it will also give him a goal. He will know he is a big boy when he does not need to wear diapers anymore.

Telling your child you used the bathroom does not need to be overly descriptive. As you walk out of the bathroom, you can look at your child and say, "Mommy went pee-pee in the potty!" Alternatively, before going into the bathroom you can say, "Daddy needs to go pee-pee; I am going to go in the potty." Making these announcements every time you or your partner goes to the bathroom will help your son realize what he needs to do. It also will make it a part of normal family discussion. It is important for your toddler to learn that the potty is just another part of normal daily activity. It is not something meant to be funny or embarrassing.

Another way to teach your toddler about what he needs to be doing is to allow him to be in the bathroom with parents or siblings. Allowing your toddler to be in the bathroom will help him to learn the process of sitting on the toilet, flushing the toilet, and washing his hands. It will also show him you are not in the bathroom to play, read, or do other things. You do what you need to do, and you leave the room. This particular tactic is emphasized in some of the potty training methods discussed in the following chapters.

When allowing toddlers in the bathroom, it is important to keep two things in mind. First, before allowing the toddler in the bathroom with a sibling, make sure his sibling is OK with that. Even young kids might feel embarrassed about having a younger sibling in the bathroom with them. Second, avoid having toddlers see boys peeing standing up. This might confuse toddlers who are getting ready to potty train. This is also why it is beneficial for young boys to be in the bathroom with their moms because they will see that they need to sit while going potty. If a boy is in the bathroom with his father, his father can either chose to sit while peeing to avoid confusion or tell his son each time that when he is big he will get to pee standing up, too. Although toddlers may resist in some areas, they do understand the difference between things little kids are allowed to do and things big people are allowed to do.

The Potty Education

Even though you might be waiting for your child subtly to let you know he is ready to begin the potty training process, you can take steps to introduce your child to the concept of the potty and encourage those signs of readiness in him. Children generally are eager to learn and gain independence. Convincing your child that being potty trained is a necessary step on the path to becoming a big kid will give him the motivation he needs to make the transition. Doing this may involve letting your toddler know that once he is potty trained, he will get to wear big kid underwear.

Getting your toddler to understand what the potty is will be one of the first challenges. If your toddler does not understand what he is expected to do while in the bathroom, he might think it is just special time he gets to spend with you. You can do several things to help your child understand what he needs to do while in the bathroom. The first is to talk about the potty often. The second is to read him lots of potty storybooks. Children might not understand everything you say the first time, but if you consistently talk about going potty, your toddler will remember the things you say.

The third thing is to not say or do things that will confuse the child. For example, avoid letting your child spend time in the bathroom playing. If your child is interested in going into the bathroom before potty training, let him in there to wash his hands, sit with you while you use the potty, or flush the toilet for you after you are finished. These activities will reinforce what goes on in the bathroom. It is important for your child to understand the bathroom is a room with a specific purpose. Do not place potty chairs in front of the television or let your child sit on the chair to do things other than try to go potty, such as eat or drink. Doing this might lead your child to thinking the potty chair is just another chair. To keep your child occupied while sitting on the potty chair, read him potty books, talk to him, or sing songs with him. One-on-one attention will encourage your child to stay on the potty chair.

Talking about the potty

You can start talking about the potty when your child is still young, even an infant. The more you talk about the potty, the more interested he will become. You can talk several ways about the potty. For example, every time you change his diaper, talk about what he did in the diaper, namely whether he peed or pooped. Tell him pee makes his diaper wet. When you start potty training, this will help him recognize that peeing makes his underwear wet.

It is also important to let your child know that everyone pees and poops. Until your toddler fully understands what is happening, using the potty might be a serious experience, especially regarding poop. Toddlers see something real and solid, and it is something they made. Remind your toddler that everyone poops, and remind family members to either allow the toddler in the bathroom with them while they poop or tell your toddler about it once they are finished. One of the potty storybooks listed in the next section is called *Everyone Poops*. This is a great book to read to your toddler so he knows his poop is not bad or gross; it is something everyone does.

Talking about the potty throughout the day will help take the mystery away from it. While talking or playing with your son, you can mention casually that one day he will not be wearing diapers anymore; he will be going pee and poop in the potty. If your son has older siblings or cousins he sees regularly, you can point out that these older kids do not wear diapers because they go in the potty. Repeatedly reminding him of this over time will make the transition out of diapers seem more natural.

Toddlers often are eager to be "big kids." This is especially true if they have older siblings or close relatives who get to do big kid things. Constantly reminding your toddler that going pee and poop in the potty is a big-kid activity will encourage and motivate him to go in the potty. Remind your toddler you use the potty and his other adult relatives use the potty. Toddlers often imitate adults and older children they look up to; this desire to imitate easily can be worked into potty training. The more excited your toddler is about potty training, the more eager he will be to go along with it.

Reading potty storybooks

In addition to talking about going to the potty, reading potty storybooks can significantly help your child learn about the potty and what he is supposed to be doing in the bathroom. Children often can understand and relate to storybooks because of the simple language and colorful pictures. The use of pictures will help your child understand the message, and listening to storybooks is a fun way for children to learn. Reading potty storybooks is also a great way to introduce potty training before you are actually ready to start potty training.

Start reading your children potty storybooks for months before introducing the potty. That way, when you do introduce the potty, it will not be completely foreign to your toddler. He will recognize it from his storybooks. There are potty storybooks that specifically address boys and girls separately. There are also books that use animals as a way of addressing potty training without dealing with gender differences. Potty storybooks can be found at libraries, so it is not necessary to spend a great deal of money buying books. Buy or borrow a variety of different potty books so your child hears about potty training in a variety of different ways.

Having an assortment of potty training books also will keep your child from getting bored with one. Reading these books to your child will give you plenty of opportunity to talk about the potty. If you are reading a potty storybook that uses a different vocabulary than the words you have chosen to use during potty training, you can change the words as you read. In addition to reading the story, you can talk about the pictures and what is going on in the pictures. You also can tell your child how the actions in the pictures apply to him. Try to choose books with a main character that is the same gender as your child. Many potty storybooks use animal characters with no specified gender. These are helpful and perfectly OK, but also include some gender-specific books. These will help your toddler identify with the main character.

Great potty training books for children

- ☆ *A Potty for Me!* by Karen Katz
- ☆ *Big Girls Use the Potty!* by Andrea Pinnington
- ☆ *Have You Seen My Potty?* by Mij Kelly and Mary McQuillan
- ☆ *Dora's Potty Book* (Dora the Explorer) by Melissa Torres and A&J Studios
- ☆ *Everyone Poops* by Taro Gomi and Amanda Mayer Stinchecum
- ☆ *Even Firefighters Go to the Potty: A Potty Training Lift-the-Flap Story* by Wendy Wax, Naomi Wax, and Stephen Gilpin
- ☆ *It Hurts When I Poop! A Story for Children Who Are Scared to Use the Potty* by Howard J., M.D. Bennett, and M. S. Weber
- ☆ *The New Potty* by Mercer Mayer and Gina Mayer
- ☆ *How to Potty Train Your Monster* by Kelly S. Dipucchio and Michael Moon
- ☆ *Potty Poo-Poo Wee-Wee!* by Colin McNaughton

Vocabulary matters

Before initiating potty training, it is important to decide what words you are going to use when referring to pee and poop. You need to choose words you will be comfortable saying and words you will be comfortable with your child repeating, even when he is in public. Once your child is using the potty and goes in public, it is common for children to talk freely about their new activities with others or to loudly announce they need to go pee or poop while in a store. It is important that you and your child's other caregivers are all comfortable using the same words.

If you refer to pee as pee-pee, but then your babysitter asks your son if he needs to "go wet," it is likely your son will not know what the babysitter is talking about. Confusing your toddler by using different terms for the same actions can lead to accidents because the toddler might get confused in regards to what is expected of him. It is also important to decide what words you want to use to refer to your child's genitals, discussed in the next section.

Avoid using the word "potty" for too many different things. For example, you can use the word "potty" when referring to the bathroom itself, or you can use the word "potty" when referring to the action of going to the bathroom. Decide if you are going to use the word "potty" as a noun or a verb, and then be consistent. If your child associates the word potty as the bathroom, then saying "go potty" might lead your toddler to think you want him to simply go into the bathroom. However, if you say, "go pee pee in the potty" it is clear what you want him to do and where you want him to do it. Young children are more likely to take what people say literally, so it is important to be as clear as possible.

List of Suggestions for Potty-Related Words

☆ Pee   ☆ Poo-poo   ☆ Number 2

☆ Pee-pee   ☆ BM   ☆ Poopy

☆ Wee-wee   ☆ Number 1   ☆ Wet

☆ Poop

Introducing the genitals

It is important to decide what words you are going to use when referencing your child's genitals because these are the same words your child is going to use while potty training. As with choosing words for pee and poop, you need to choose words you are going to be comfortable using. You will need to say these words when telling your child how to clean him or herself. In addition, if your child is having trouble or something hurts, you want him to be able to accurately communicate the problem to you. It is important that you can use these words with your toddler without getting embarrassed or flustered. Showing embarrassment may confuse your toddler and lead him to believe he should feel embarrassed when talking about genitals.

Some doctors and parents advocate using the proper terms when referring to genitals. This means you would teach your son to use the word penis, as opposed to "wee-wee" or "privates." However, many parents are not comfortable using these words with their young children, and there is no medically researched advantage to using the technical terms. It is important to use words you are comfortable with because you do not want to make your toddler feel as though he should be embarrassed by saying the same words.

One major issue most parents will face at some point is their child's interest in touching his genitals. This is completely normal, and it is important not to overreact. Overreacting to this type of behavior will either make your child feel he should be embarrassed about his body or it will encourage him to do it more. It is not abnormal for toddlers to do things solely because they know they can get a big reaction out of their parents. To discourage the behavior, calmly distract them from what they are doing. It is also important to remind your toddler the importance of cleanliness. *This will be discussed in detail in Chapter 4.* Remind your toddler how important it is to keep his hands clean, and have him wash his hands.

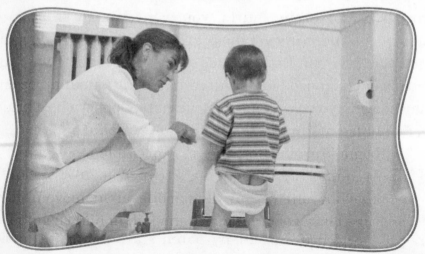

List of suggestions for words referring to body parts

Alternate words for butt

☆ Bottom
☆ Bum
☆ Tush
☆ Derriere
☆ Rear
☆ Caboose
☆ Fanny
☆ Behind
☆ Hiney
☆ Hind-end
☆ Rump
☆ Tookus

Alternate words for penis

☆ Wee-wee (do not use to mean both pee and penis)
☆ Pee-pee (do not use to mean both pee and penis)
☆ Privates
☆ Weiner

Alternate words for vagina

☆ Business
☆ Privates
☆ Bottom (do not use bottom to mean both butt and vagina)
☆ Tinkle or tinker
☆ Tota

Go Shopping

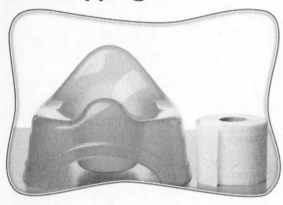

A list of needed items will be included with each potty training method described. The exact items you need will vary depending on the potty training method you choose.

However, some of the items you need no matter what. For example, hand soap and sanitizer, some sort or potty seat or potty chair, and potty training picture books will be needed regardless of who you potty train or at what age you start potty training. In addition to these items, you will need to make sure your bathroom is stocked with all the normal essentials, such as toilet paper and hand towels. If your child is unable to reach the toilet paper dispenser, you can either purchase a toilet paper extender, have a loose roll sitting closer to the toilet specifically for your child to use, or teach your child to get off the potty before wiping.

Potty chairs and potty seats — What is best?

The practicality and comfort of a potty chair versus a potty seat placed on an adult toilet is relative. Whichever is used for potty training is what your toddler will be used to for the first several months or years after potty training. This can lead to difficulties using public toilets at first. Your child might be afraid of failing if he is accustomed to sitting on a potty chair with both feet firmly on the ground. One way to deal with this is to crouch down in front of your child while he sits on the toilet so he can see your face and have both your hands firmly on his waist. You also can carry a traveling toilet seat with you at all times. This may help your child feel more secure while sitting on a bigger toilet. If your child is still resistant or scared to use a public toilet, you will need to schedule outings around potty breaks. Always carry extra clothes and baby wipes in case your child has an accident. Your child will be ready to transition from the potty chair or potty seat to a regular toilet seat when he learns to hold himself up while going to the bathroom. You either can teach your child to lean forward while sitting on the toilet so his body weight is holding him toward the edge of the toilet seat, or you can teach your child to hold himself up by placing both hands on either side of the toilet seat while he sits. If you have chosen an early potty training method, you will be firmly holding your child whether he is on a potty chair or a potty seat. However, for early potty training, a potty chair will be easier for your baby to adjust to as he learns to sit on the potty by himself.

Potty chairs

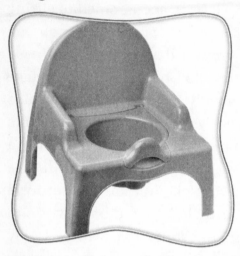

Buying a potty chair is an important step in potty training. You want to get one that is comfortable, easy to use, easy to empty and clean, and fun. However, you do not want it to be too much fun. There are potty chairs available that talk and play music. Although these seem appealing, they might be more of a distraction than a motivation. For some children, a musical potty chair might be enticing, but these chairs are more expensive than plain potty chairs, and you will not be able to return a used potty chair if you do discover it is too much of a distraction for your child. Your son should want to sit on the potty chair, but you do not want him to play with the potty chair. Playing with the potty chair might lead your toddler to seeing the chair as one of his toys, which might distract him from actually using it to go pee and poop.

Some potty chairs look like actual chairs, and some look like miniature toilets. Some potty chairs look like thrones, and some potty chairs have cartoon characters on them. Although all these potty chairs look fun and your child might like them, they are not necessary. This is not to say you should not buy them; just know the plain, solid-colored, plastic one will work just fine. Most potty chairs are not padded; they are hard plastic. You can use either hard or padded potty chairs; both can be used effectively to potty train.

Even if you are using a potty chair for training, it is still important to have your child practice flushing the regular toilet and know how other people use the regular toilet. Although the potty chair can be very beneficial during training, the ultimate goal is still to have the child transition to the regular toilet once potty trained. The point of transition is different for different children. However, as a rule, once your child is predictably dry throughout the day and initiating potty use on his own, it is time to suggest he try sitting on the toilet when he needs to go pee or poop. Most children are eager to do things they see adults doing, so in most cases the transition is seamless. *Helping your child adjust to the adult toilet will be covered more in Chapter 14.*

There is a significant cost difference in potty chairs. A plain potty chair costs between $10.50 and $19.99, while the more elaborate potty chairs cost between $24.99 and $69.99. If you want a fun potty chair but cannot afford it, consider getting the plain one and then decorating it with stickers. This could be a fun activity for you and your child to do together in preparation for its use. It will get him excited about the chair, and if he had a hand in decorating it, he might be happier about seeing it used. Anything that helps encourage your toddler to embrace using the potty chair will be helpful.

If you do choose to buy a potty seat, a good way to introduce your child to it is to let him pick out his own potty chair. If he chooses a potty that comes with a deflector, take it off before he sits on it. The deflector is designed to prevent boys from peeing all over the bathroom. However, they are rigid and placed right at the front of the potty chair, which makes it to easy for a little boy to scrape his privates against it while sitting down. If this happens, your son will be unlikely to want to sit on the potty anymore. To prevent him from peeing up and out of the potty chair, teach him to sit all the way back and push his penis down before he starts to pee. If you are potty training a little girl, the deflector is unnecessary, and little girls can scrape their privates against it as well, so it should be removed.

However, buying a potty chair is not a strict requirement for potty training. The advantages of using a potty chair are that they are low to the ground, easy to use, easy to empty, and easy to clean. They also can be placed anywhere in the house, which is an advantage if the bathroom is not an ideal location. However, they are an additional cost, and they take up space, which you might not have. Finally, potty chairs need to be cleaned out every time they are used, as opposed to potty seats, which allow the pee and poop to fall directly into the toilet.

Potty seats

Potty seats are cushioned toilet seats that are placed right on top of the toilet seat. They are secure, so the child will not slide off the toilet, and they make the opening in the seat smaller, so the child does not feel as if he is going to fall in the toilet. Even if you are holding the child,

if he feels as if he might fall, he will be too tense to pee or poop. Children need to feel relaxed in order to loosen their muscles enough to pee and poop.

The advantages to using a potty seat are that they are relatively small, they are easy to move, and they travel easily. Although regular potty seats are small enough to travel, if you are tight on space, you also can buy a traveling potty seat. A traveling potty seat is the same as a regular potty seat, except it can be folded to one quarter the normal size. This will allow you to keep the potty seat in a gallon-sized bag in your carry-on. The main disadvantage of a potty seat is that it sits on top of the toilet seat, which means your child still either will need to be lifted onto the toilet or learn to get up on the toilet by himself.

Adult toilets with a potty seat can be a little scary because the child is higher off the ground and might be afraid of falling. One way to combat the fear of falling is by buying a potty seat with handles. This will allow the child to hold onto the seat while he sits on the toilet and will make him feel more secure. Also, you will have to keep a small step stool in the bathroom for your child to use when he needs to sit on the toilet. Otherwise, you will have to be there to lift him securely onto the toilet each time.

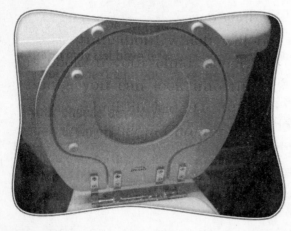 Potty seats might be more practical if your bathroom is too small for a potty chair to be comfortably located in. It is important to keep in mind that potty seats need to be removed in order for an adult to use the toilet. This means the potty seat will likely be put on the floor next to the toilet between uses. And you will need room for the step stool. If these items will not fit in your bathroom either, you might need to consider putting a potty chair in a different part of the house.

There is one further option for potty seats. You can buy an adult toilet seat with a toddler seat attached. The toddler toilet seat is embedded in the lid of the adult toilet seat and is held in place by a magnet. When the toddler needs to use the toilet, the seat easily can be pulled down. To put the seat back up, you just need to close the

**PHOTOS COURTESY OF
WWW.CRYSTALRIVERHOUSE.COM**

lid and then reopen it. When the lid closes, the magnet will draw the toddler toilet seat back into its place.

Hand soap

The bathroom always should be well stocked with hand soap, and the hand soap should be easily accessible. Teaching your child to wash his hands properly every time he is in the bathroom is an essential part of potty training. While teaching your toddler how to wash his hands, it might be helpful to buy foaming hand soap. This will prevent your toddler from using too much soap and making a soapy mess. You also might want to buy antibacterial hand sanitizer to use as well while your toddler is being trained and immediately after training. Your child will be coming in contact with his own pee and poop while learning how to use the bathroom and clean himself. Antibacterial hand sanitizer will help to minimize the spread of germs during this process.

Step stool

Having a step stool in the bathroom is useful for two things. The first use is for washing your child's hands because using a footstool will allow your toddler to reach the hand soap easily and the faucet without help. Although, at first, you will be with your child while he is washing his hands, he should be able to do it himself. The second thing a stool is useful for is for your child to use when getting onto the toilet and sitting on it. If your toddler's feet are dangling, he will not be able to relax his muscles enough to poop comfortably. Letting him keep his feet on a footstool while going the bathroom will help him significantly, and it will make going to the bathroom more comfortable.

Big kid underpants

Transitioning from diapers to big kid underpants is a significant move for toddlers. Buy two types of big kid underpants: padded training underpants and regular child underpants. The padded underpants will be helpful in dealing with accidents the first couple of days of potty training. However, unlike diapers that hold moisture away from your child, the cloth training underwear will get wet and uncomfortable every time he pees or poops, which will encourage him to use the potty instead of treating his pants as a diaper. If you are concerned with your child having an accident while sitting on the furniture or on other surfaces that are not easy to clean, you can have your child wear plastic pants over top of the cloth training underwear. Plastic pants look just like diaper covers, but they are made of plastic, so they will help to hold in any mess from an accident. Once your child understands what he needs to do and is letting you know when he needs to pee or poop, you can move him to regular kid underpants.

Avoid using disposable training pants. Although they slide on and off like underpants, they still feel like diapers. In addition, there will be no consequence for your toddler if he does have an accident. Although it might create a temporarily uncomfortable situation, it is important for your toddler to be aware immediately when he has an accident. Finally, disposable training pants are expensive and do nothing to speed up the potty training process.

Doll, fake poop, and fake pee

Another good method in teaching children about going to the potty is to use visuals, in this case, a doll. To do this, you will need a doll that has removable clothes. Although there are dolls that go pee and poop on their own, it is best to use a regular doll that can be undressed. If you use a regular doll, you will be able to control when it pees and poops by putting fake pee or poop in the potty chair or toilet when you are ready for the doll to go. Dolls that do it on their own might make it difficult for you to get the doll to go pee and poop in the toddler toilet because the dolls use the bathroom at random times, not on demand. *The method of using a potty training doll is explained in detail in Chapter 5.* On the first day of potty training, you will help your toddler potty train his doll as an introduction to potty training. Potty training dolls can be used with both boys and girls. If your son does not want to use a doll, you can also use a teddy bear or other stuffed animal.

If using a doll as a visual and teaching aid, you will need to have fake poop and pee ready for the first day of potty training. You do not need to buy fake pee or poop. You can use lemonade or a lemon juice mix for the fake pee. You also will need a dropper or small squeeze bottle to put the fake pee in the potty while your toddler is potty training his doll or stuffed animal. For fake poop, you can use strained prunes. You will need to distract your toddler temporary while you put the fake poop in the potty, but it will be convincing, especially if your toddler has never seen strained prunes. One easy way to distract the child is to make sure the toilet paper is behind your child, and then ask him to get a piece of toilet paper for the doll.

Potty storybooks and videos

Earlier in the chapter, you were provided with a list of titles for potty storybooks. Potty storybooks can be introduced months before you actually begin potty training. The earlier you start reading potty storybooks, the better understanding your child will have before the start of potty training. It is also important to have multiple potty storybooks on hand while you are potty training. Reading potty

storybooks will be a good activity to do throughout the first and second day of potty training. You also can get potty training videos for your child to watch. These videos, like the storybooks, use child-friendly characters and stories to teach children how to use the potty. If the videos you picked out use vocabulary that is different from the vocabulary you have chosen to use during potty training, you can translate the words for your child while you are watching the video together. For example, let us say you have decided to use the phrase "tinkle" for when you child needs to pee, but the video you picked out uses the phrase "pee-pee." Each time the characters in the video say "pee-pee," you can say to your child, "She's talking about needing to go tinkle."

Monetary Expenses

Although there are expenses related to potty training, the cost is minimal when compared to the ongoing cost of diapers. The costs are also one-time or temporary. Potty training is inevitable, so putting it off because of the cost of training supplies is not going to save you money. That being said, there are some costs to consider. If the cost of potty training supplies is an issue, there are ways to lessen the expenses, which also will be discussed.

Taking off work

You can avoid taking time off work by either choosing a method designed to work in just a couple days or by choosing a method that does not require you to take away the diapers completely. If you are using a method that should only take a couple of days, you can start potty training on a Saturday morning and continue through Sunday. Whether potty training will need to extend into Monday will depend on how the weekend went. Even if your toddler is not potty trained by Monday, a well-informed babysitter or family member could handle the rest of the process. If you are using a method that does not require you to take away the diapers completely, you can work on potty training while you are at home and put your child in diapers while you are at work. Either way, getting your toddler's caregivers involved in the process will make it go faster and eliminate the need for you to take time off of work.

The cost of the items needed

The cost of needed items will vary depending on brand or style. It is important to know that only the basic items are needed. For example, more expensive potty seats will not potty train your toddler any faster than plain-looking, less expensive ones. Potty chairs will range in price from $10 to $70. Potty training seats, the ones that will fit on a standard toilet seat, will range in price from $10 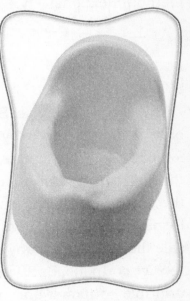 to $33. Potty step stools range in price from $12 to $60. Finally, thick training underpants cost approximately $7 for three pairs, and regular toddler size underpants cost approximately $11 for seven pairs.

Ways to save money

When you add everything up, the cost of potty training supplies can be significant. Despite the fact that potty training is necessary, for many people, the additional cost of potty training supplies is significant. However, you can use a variety of tactics to save money on the temporary costs of potty training. These tactics include saving and using coupons, sharing items, using hand-me-down items, and cutting corners. Regardless of the potty training method you chose to follow, there are ways to follow the method inexpensively.

Coupons

Often, stores such as Babies R Us and Target that offer baby registries and baby supply departments offer coupons for parents. You can register to be on their mailing lists through their websites, and then coupons will be sent to you through the mail and email, depending on your preference. Registered parents regularly receive coupon packets and sale fliers on their baby and toddler items. It is common to receive coupons for 20 percent off one item. You can collect multiple coupons, and use one for each needed item. Ask family members to get on the mailing list to ensure you will have access to multiple coupons when they are sent out. You also can look for online offers. Often, stores like Target and Babies R Us will have great offers or clearance items available only through their websites.

Sharing potty items with friends

Another simple way to save money is to share potty training items or be open to hand-me-down items. The nice thing about potty chairs and training seats is they are made completely from plastic and are easy to clean and sanitize. If you have a relative or friend who has recently potty trained a toddler and is willing to pass the items along, it would certainly save you money. You can check your local library for potty training storybooks and videos. These will be free to use, as long as you return them on time.

You also can check local resale shops for things such as step stools and potty chairs. Many areas have resale shops that specialize in baby and child items. Although this might not be ideal, it is a possibility. Watch your local newspapers for a kids' resale event. Many moms' groups and preschool PTAs will have annual kids' resale events as fundraisers. These events allow parents to set up tables and sell their unneeded baby items. If you buy used potty training items, you can sanitize them easily by washing them with a bleach-based cleaning solution. You also can clean the items with hot soapy water and spray everything with a disinfectant.

Cutting corners

Another way to save money is to cut corners. As mentioned earlier, the more expensive potty training items do not potty train children any faster than the less expensive items. Make the decision to buy the cheapest possible options. Use a doll you already own for the potty doll instead of buying a new one. And skip the thicker training underpants. Although they do help absorb accidents better than regular underpants, they are not necessary. You also can go without the plastic underpants. Once again, they help lessen the mess from accidents, but they are not essential for potty training. Finally, you can train a child to use a regular adult toilet from the start. It will not be as easy, and it may extend the time it takes you to potty train, but it is possible. If you cannot afford a potty chair or seat and you cannot find a hand-me-down one, going without may be your only option.

Setting the Scene

No matter which method you choose to use to potty train your child, it would benefit you, your child, and the entire enterprise if you took steps to prepare everything the night before starting, so you can begin potty training first thing in the morning. This also will put you in the right frame of mind for potty training. Having everything set out and ready will prevent you from feeling flustered or overwhelmed in the morning. If you have older kids that need to get ready for school in the morning, make sure all their stuff is set out and ready as well. This will prevent their morning routine from being too distracting for your toddler.

The night before you are to begin potty training, place the potty chair in the area you designated for potty training. If you decided to use the toilet instead of buying a potty chair, make sure the potty seat and step stool are in place for your toddler to use. Make sure the bathroom is clean and stocked with toilet paper, soap, and hand towels. Have extra hand towels clean and ready in case you need to use the towel to clean up a mess. Set out all the potty storybooks and videos, so you are not looking for them the next day.

If you are using a doll as a prop in the potty training process, the doll you will use can be placed in your toddler's room once he is asleep. That way he will see it as soon as he wakes up, which is when the potty training will start. You also can keep the doll in your room for the night and then bring it with you when you go to wake up your toddler in the morning. Either way, you want the doll to be ready and involved first thing in the morning.

You also want to be fully prepared to execute this method without needing to refer back to this book throughout the day. Read over what you need to do, and make yourself a checklist if you are concerned you will forget. *Checklists are already prepared in the Appendix if you want a pre-existing list.* It is also important to have activities ready to do with your child throughout the day that do not involve watching television. When children are watching the television, they are often less aware of their own functioning and actions. A toddler can easily have an accident and not realize it until after the fact. Instead of watching television, be prepared with potty storybooks to read together, short games, and simple crafts. Activities that are short will give you ideal opportunities to take bathroom breaks.

What the child will wear

Once you are taking your toddler out of his diaper for potty training, you should put out soft and loosely fitting clothes for him to wear. Your child likely will know how to get dressed by himself, and this will give him a chance to practice himself and feel like a big kid in preparation for this next big step. Have your toddler wear a shirt that does not go past his waist. Having to hold up a long shirt will make it difficult for him to pull his pants up and down. For the first day of potty training, he does not need to wear pants. A child having an accident while struggling to get his pants down will cause frustration and possibly resistance in the child. In the first day or two, it is best to make the process as easy as possible by allowing the child to wear as few clothes as possible. On the second day of potty training, he can wear elastic waist pants so he can practice getting his pants and underpants on and off.

Although potty training can be completed quickly, many children might still have difficulties for weeks or even months afterward. It is important to create a situation where your toddler is not likely to have an accident. Until your child can quickly and effectively button and unbutton pants, it will be best to have him wear elastic waist pants. Jeans are often the hardest for toddlers to get on and off by themselves. You do not want your toddler to have an accident in the bathroom while trying to get undressed. Also, be careful having a little girl wear a dress. It may seem like it would be easiest to potty train in, but if it is not pulled up high enough, your daughter may end up letting the back of the dress fall in the toilet and get wet.

Mental pep talk

Once again, mental preparation is as important as all other forms of preparation. By the time you are actually ready to initiate potty training, you will have been preparing your toddler mentally for weeks. Talking about the potty, letting your toddler in the bathroom while you go potty, and reading potty storybooks are all the ways you will be preparing your toddler mentally for potty training. You also will be preparing your child mentally by consistently reminding him that big kids use the potty and do not wear diapers and by letting him know that once he starts using the potty he will get to wear big kid underpants.

Being mentally prepared also means being prepared for the unexpected or embarrassing. For example, it is common for toddlers to play with their poop. Although you might find this disgusting, it is important not to overreact. This is a common behavior for toddlers. You need to understand the situation from their point of view. To a toddler, poop is something funny and mushy that they made all by themselves. Although it is important to stop your toddler and strongly discourage the behavior, it is also important to not yell or tell your child he is gross or disgusting.

The best way for you to prepare mentally for potty training is by being prepared and being open to the experience. It is important to be confident in the potty training method you chose and confident that your child is capable of being potty trained. You also need to be flexible. For example, if your toddler wakes up sick the day you planned to start potty training, you probably should hold off until he is feeling better. It is also important to be prepared for accidents and other mishaps.

Commitment is also important once you decide it is time to potty train your toddler. Once you introduce potty training, try to avoid falling back into using diapers on a regular basis during the day. Diapers still can be useful for nighttime bed-wetting, going on long trips, or going out in public for a long period. However, if you are at home with your child, have him go without the diaper. Consistency is important for toddlers.

Because it is so important to be consistent, it is also important to be prepared for accidents. Even though the potty training process should only take a couple of days, it will take weeks or months for your child to perfect this. Keep an extra set of clothes in each of your vehicles, so you always have clothes if your toddler has an accident while you are away from the house. This will prevent unplanned trips back home, as well as creating frustration and disappointment for your child; it will also help you stay calm.

Chapter 4:
Teaching Toilet Etiquette

Toilet etiquette is an essential part of potty training. Although your primary focus is on getting your child to acknowledge when she needs to use the bathroom and use it without an accident, you still will need to incorporate all of the hygiene steps mentioned in this chapter while you are teaching potty training. It might be easy to overlook the importance of toilet etiquette. Toilet etiquette includes how a child should clean herself and how she needs to wash her hands. It also will cover how to act in a restroom and how to talk about bathroom needs while in public. Toilet etiquette also covers other issues, such as modesty, touching, and listening.

Sidebar on bathroom safety

Before potty training, many parents make the bathroom unavailable to their young children. However, once a child is being potty trained, she will need access to the bathroom. For that reason, it is important to make the bathroom a safe place for your child. Store anything that could be hazardous, such as razors, cleaners, or extra supplies. You can install a high shelf or get a lock for the bathroom cabinet. If you are unable to arrange secured storage in the bathroom, you should avoid storing medicine or cleaners in the bathroom. You also should check the temperature of your hot water tank. To prevent burning, it is recommended that the water temperature be set no higher than 120 degrees. This will prevent your child from accidentally scalding herself if she turns the faucet on the wrong way.

Wiping Lessons

According to a 2002 research study, girls are slightly older than 4 years old and boys are slightly younger than 4 years old by they time they can effectively wipe poop off themselves. These ages reflect the average, so plenty of children older than 4 are still unable to properly wipe themselves. Wiping is an important lesson, but keep in mind it is a difficult skill for children to master, which is one reason daily baths are important during this period.

Wiping lessons will be different for girls and boys. If you have a little girl, it is important to teach her the differences between wiping pee and wiping poop. It is important when a girl is wiping poop that she wipe front to back. This might be difficult at first, but it is important to reinforce this lesson continually. Wiping front to back will prevent the poop from touching her vagina and urethra, which will prevent her from getting an infection. During potty training, little girls are highly susceptible to infections due to improper cleaning. Making sure she bathes daily also will help to clean away any fecal matter or germs that were missed while wiping.

Although little boys are not susceptible to infections in the same way girls are, it is still important that they are taught to wipe away the poop after they go to the bathroom. Remaining clean will prevent rashes and preserve their underpants. While boys are being potty trained, you should have them wipe after peeing. Peeing while sitting down means it is more likely that urine and toilet water may splash on their skin. *The differences in dealing with circumcised boys and uncircumcised boys will be discussed in Chapter 12.*

While you are still going into the bathroom with your toddler each time, show her how much toilet paper to take off the roll, and then, show her how to wipe. After the first couple times, let her do it, but monitor her actions closely. It is common for children to use far too much toilet paper. This can cause clogged toilets and wasted toilet paper. Although this might cause some frustration, it is important to keep reinforcing how much toilet paper she needs and how she needs to wipe. Eventually, she will be able to clean herself properly without using a large amount of toilet paper.

Hand Washing Lessons

Proper hand washing is important. A wide variety of germs and diseases can be spread through pee and poop. When children do not properly wash their hands, the pee and poop that might have gotten on their hands is spread to everything they touch. When other people touch those same things, the germs continue to be spread. Hand washing is the easiest way to reduce the spread of germs and disease.

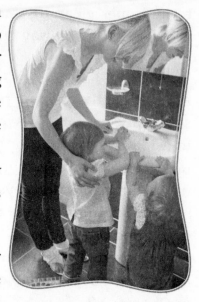

When you are teaching your child to wash her hands, have her turn the water on first and get her hands a little wet. Instruct her to put some soap on her hands. Then, she needs to rub her hands together to get the soap all over. Demonstrate for her how to wash her palms, the back of her hands, her fingers, and in between her fingers. Wash your hands with her, so she can see how well you wash your hands. Choose a song to sing while you are washing hands. For example, singing "Happy Birthday" is easy enough for a toddler to learn but long enough to allow thorough hand washing. When the song is over, rinse the soap off your hands, and dry them with a clean towel.

Although at first, you will be there to turn the water on, it is important to teach your toddler to turn the water on with her elbow, or if that is not possible, keep napkins in the bathroom. Teach your child to turn the faucet on with a napkin in her hand to keep the pee and poop from getting on the faucet. It is also important to teach your toddler how the warm and cold water come on. You want your child to learn to wash her hands with warm water.

Effective Communication between Parent and Child

Ideally, before initiating potty training, you chose the terms you wanted to use, and you have taught them to your toddler. This will be important for your toddler to be able to let you know effectively that she needs to go pee or poop. Communication between parent and child is essential to successful potty training. In addition to the need to use the bathroom, you will need to communicate specific instructions verbally to your child. For example, you will need to teach your child how to wipe herself with toilet paper and explain to her why it is important to keep her privates clean. After wiping herself, instruct your toddler to drop the toilet paper into the toilet without touching it excessively. If you are using a potty chair, pour the contents of the chair into the toilet. This will reinforce in your child's mind that pee and poop belongs in the toilet. Finally, instruct her to flush the toilet after she is completely done wiping herself.

Parent/child communication refers to how well the parents communicate information to the child. Parents need to remember the age of the child they potty training. Everything should be explained slowly and calmly. Parents need to get down to their toddler's level by kneeling on the floor. It is also important to make eye contact when talking to your toddler. This will help her stay focused on what you are saying. Finally, parents should frequently ask their toddler if she understands what is being said. Stay with your child throughout the entire process of going potty to provide instruction along the way. This includes hand washing. While demonstrating how to wash hands properly, explain to your child how to avoid getting soap and water all over the bathroom counter.

Child/parent communication refers to how well your child communicates with you. Depending on the age of your child when you begin potty training, verbal communication might not be very developed. However, it is not needed if your child can communicate effectively without it. In order to avoid misunderstandings, it is important to repeat back to your child what you think she said to you. For example, if you are sure your daughter said she needed to pee, you can ask, "Do you need to go pee?" Repeat back everything your child says to reinforce the communication and to give your child a chance to try again if you misunderstood her.

Nonverbal communication

It is also important to be able to read your toddler's nonverbal communication. Young children sometimes do not communicate verbally their need to go to the bathroom until it is too late and an accident is unavoidable. This is especially true if she is distracted watching television or playing a game and does not want to stop what she is doing. It is also more common for toddlers to have accidents while they are playing outside. They do  not want to stop playing, and by the time they do stop, it is too late for them to get to a bathroom. To avoid these types of accidents, parents can watch for nonverbal cues that their toddler needs to go to the bathroom. The following is a list of common things children will do when they need to go to the bathroom:

- ☆ Shift their weight back and forth
- ☆ Pace
- ☆ Grab their genitals
- ☆ Hop up and down
- ☆ Stand with their legs tightly together
- ☆ Squat for extended periods
- ☆ Cross their legs while standing
- ☆ Do the "potty dance," which is often a combination of shifting their weight and hopping up and down

Effective listening and verbalizing from both you and your toddler will reduce the number of accidents greatly and expedite the potty training process. Taking the time to listen to your child and speaking in calm, clear sentences are as important as your child learning how to communicate her need to use the bathroom. It often takes young children a few seconds or longer to get out what they are trying to say. It is important that parents give their toddlers the opportunity to put their thoughts into words. Rewarding your child with praise after effectively listening or verbalizing will reinforce that behavior.

Appropriate Behavior

Once a child has been introduced to potty training, it will be important to teach your toddler how to act in public restrooms. For an extended time, you will need to be in the same stall as your toddler. It is important to teach your toddler that she should not sit down on the bathroom floor or crawl under stall doors. She should not try to see or talk to people in other stalls, and she should not try to open the stall door before you are both finished using the bathroom. Although you do not want to scare your child, it is important to teach her that public restrooms might be dirty, and it is important to wash her hands well.

Another issue you might run into is needing to take a girl into the men's room or a boy into the ladies' room. Some small businesses might only have a single private bathroom similar to a home bathroom. Many businesses

are moving toward offering "family bathrooms," which are single bathrooms designed to be used by men or women, and they are larger, so if you need to take multiple children into the bathroom with you, you can. However, if a family bathroom is not available, fathers will need to take girls into the men's room, and mothers will need to take boys into the women's room. Women's restrooms have all stalls with doors, so everything is private. However, men's restrooms often have urinals out in the open. If a father needs to take a little girl into the men's room with him, he can check first and wait until no one is at the urinals, or he can carry her into one of the stalls and make sure she is turned away from the men at the urinals. Although having to take a child into an opposite gender bathroom might be uncomfortable, if there are no other options, it is better than forcing your child to have an accident. Another way to avoid this situation is to make sure your child goes to the bathroom before leaving the house and make trips to places without family bathrooms short. If you are making several stops, be sure to take advantage of the businesses that offer family bathrooms or single bathrooms.

Another issue you need to face concerning public restrooms is your child wanting to go to the bathroom alone. As long as your child still needs help either going to the bathroom, wiping, or washing hands, you need to be there every step of the way. However, once your child is able to manage going to the bathroom alone, you can start to back off. There is no set age professionals agree is the appropriate age for a child to be alone in a public restroom. However, you will need to make sure your child can manage alone by the time she starts school. You can ease into this by allowing her to go into a stall by herself. Once you are comfortable knowing she can manage by herself in a stall, you can back off more by allowing her to go into a bathroom alone but with you standing right by the door. Tell her to call for you if she needs help. This is appropriate for small public restrooms that only have one door leading in and out. If the restroom is large, such as those in an airport, movie theater, or stadium, or if there are multiple doors, you should stay with your child for her safety.

Modesty

Although toddlers are not old enough to understand what modesty is or why it is important, potty training is an ideal time to introduce the concept. This is as simple as explaining to your toddler that some things are private. For example, children often want to keep the bathroom door open while using the bathroom. Once your toddler is potty trained to the point that you let her go in the bathroom alone, you can tell her that she needs privacy when she is using the potty, and she should close the door. This is an important lesson for when you have company over or when you are in a public restroom. If your child needs help, encourage her to ask you to come in the bathroom as opposed to coming out into the living area undressed.

Touching

Another issue you likely will need to deal with is touching. Wearing big kid underpants feels different from wearing a diaper, and often toddlers start touching their genitals a lot. This kind of behavior is not restricted to boys. Little girls also will be more inclined to start touching themselves once they are in underwear. Avoid overreacting to the behavior, but discourage your child from doing it. Touching her genitals and then touching other things without washing her hands will spread germs. In addition, little kids can hurt themselves unintentionally. Little girls and boys can accidentally scratch themselves if their fingernails are not short enough or are filed unevenly. Finally, touching is strongly discouraged once your child enters preschool, and even more so in kindergarten. Getting your toddler out of the habit before it goes too far will avoid a potentially uncomfortable conference with her teacher.

The best way to discourage this behavior is through consistent and constant reminders. Be gentle with your child, but firm in reminding her that she should not touch her private parts unless she is washing. Every time you see your child touching herself, calmly tell her to stop touching and instruct her to go wash her hands. Having her wash her hands will reinforce the idea that cleanliness and good hygiene is important. If your toddler is starting school, inform the teacher that you are working on correcting this behavior. You do not want your child to get into trouble at school for a bad habit.

Chapter 5:
The One-Day Potty Party Method

T
There are two versions of the one-day method. Although both versions are parent-centered approaches, the potty party method is a more caring and fun approach to parent-centered potty training. The first version of the method had some clear disadvantages, which led to the development of the potty party method. Although both versions of the one-day method promote getting your child potty trained in one day, the potty party method is more enjoyable for your child. Even if your child is not completely potty trained in one day using this method, your child should be mostly potty trained if you followed the method correctly. Your child might still experience isolated accidents but should be dependably dry.

Development of the Method

Dr. Nathan Azrin and Dr. Richard Foxx first introduced the one-day approach to potty training in the early 1970s. Their method involves constant repetition and reinforcement, and it uses a potty training doll. Azrin and Foxx instruct parents to help their toddler potty train a doll and then potty train himself. To potty train the doll, parents would have their child check the doll's clothes every five minutes to see if they are dry. Once the child establishes that the doll's clothes are dry, the parents would then suggest the child take the doll to the bathroom to see if it needs to go pee or poop. Following the training, parents should have their toddler do a dry test every five minutes. This involves having your toddler feel his underpants to see if they are wet or dry. If his underpants are dry, he gets a small treat. If he is wet, you are instructed to show your disapproval of the accident, make him go into the bathroom and practice going on the potty the right way, and then, he has to take responsibility for the accident by cleaning it up. Azrin and Foxx instruct parents to have the toddler change out of the wet or soiled underpants, take them to the designated laundry area, get new clean underpants, and then, clean up any mess. That means if the child peed and got pee on the floor, you should give him a rag and have him clean up the wet spot on the floor.

The primary benefit of this method is that if it works, your toddler will be potty trained in one day. In addition, the method is based on repetition and reinforcement, which are proven methods of training for young children. However, the method does put a great deal of pressure on both the parents and the toddler. According to Azrin and Foxx, it took the average child only four hours to be completely potty trained. During their study, they had children potty trained in as little as 30 minutes. On the other hand, they also noted that the longest it took to potty train a child during their study was two 14-hour days. A 14-hour day is a long day for both the parents and the toddler. This method is intensive, and it sets parents up to feel bad if they are not able to potty train their child in less than a day. A great deal of pressure placed is on the parents and the toddler following this method. Finally, having a child clean up his own pee and poop creates a cleanliness issue. The toddler will need to have his hands thoroughly washed, and the floor will need to be cleaned again with a bleach-based cleaner or sprayed with a disinfectant.

Since Azrin and Foxx introduced the one-day method, others have altered the method to suit different needs. For example, from this method came the potty party method. The potty party method follows a basic one-day method but combines the basic method with a party atmosphere. Although the goal is still to potty train your child in one day, the day is spent having fun. Both you and your child will be relaxed and excited about potty training. Several child-care professionals and psychologists have expanded and promoted the potty party method as a fun and successful means of potty training.

How to Prepare

This particular method requires a lot of preparation. You will need to prepare your child for potty training by talking about it regularly and either allowing your child into the bathroom while you are going or letting your child watch potty training videos and read potty storybooks in the weeks leading up to your day of potty training. Doing both will provide the most reinforcement. In addition to preparing your child, you will need to prepare logistically for the potty party. A potty party may take days or even weeks to plan, depending on how involved you want the party to be.

What you will need

☆ Party decorations
☆ Potty chair or potty seat
☆ Doll or appropriate stuffed animal
☆ Clothes for the doll
☆ Fake pee
☆ Fake poop
☆ Lots of good beverages
☆ Gifts
☆ Sticker chart for the doll
☆ Sticker chart for your child
☆ Potty storybooks
☆ Short potty training videos

The night before

The night before the potty party, tell your child you have a fun day planned, and explain to him that he will pot train the chosen doll the next day. Tell him that the two of you will have a potty party together. You want your child to be excited about the potty party, but not so excited that he does not sleep. Being well rested will make the day go much better for both of you.

After your child goes to bed for the night, you need to prepare for the party. Although you do not need to prepare extravagant decorations, you want to have a fun party atmosphere. Your focus for decorations should be the bathroom you intend to use for potty training and the living space where you plan to spend the time you are not in the bathroom. It is important to have the potty seat or potty chair set  up and ready when your toddler gets up the next morning. This can be the living room, playroom, or family room, for example. In this room, you will want to set out the potty training storybooks and games you plan to play.

You also will need to wrap the gifts you got for your child. You will give him some of the gifts at lunch after he potty trains the doll and some of the gifts at dinner after he is potty trained. You also will need to have the doll ready with a change of clothes. You will need to have the fake pee and poop ready and easily accessible. You will need to be able to get to it without your child noticing. Finally, hang the two sticker charts on the bathroom door where they will be noticeable.

Time to Potty Train

The day of the potty party is separated into two parts: morning and afternoon. In the morning, your child will be potty training his doll; in the afternoon, he will be potty training himself. Wake your child up first thing in the morning for the potty party. Get him dressed in his party clothes and explain to him he will be potty training his doll today. Make sure he is drinking plenty of liquids all morning and afternoon during all the activities so he will have to go in the afternoon. After breakfast, take him and the doll into the bathroom. Show him how to lower the doll's pants and sit the doll on the potty. Show your son the doll's sticker chart and tell him that the doll will get a sticker every time the doll goes pee-pee or poop in the potty. Then, go back to the living room with the doll to play a short game or read a couple potty storybooks.

Every five to ten minutes, remind your child to take the doll to the bathroom. On these trips, have your child put the doll on the potty, after asking him where the doll should sit. When you go into the bathroom, have an eyedropper ready with lemonade in it. Distract your child just long enough to squirt some of the lemonade into the potty by asking him to get you toilet paper or get a sticker ready for the sticker chart. Then, have him check to see if the doll went pee-pee. He will see the lemonade and think the doll did go pee-pee in the potty. Have him get a small piece of toilet paper and show him how to wipe the doll. Instruct him to drop the toilet paper into the adult toilet. Then, help him pour the contents of the potty chair into the adult toilet if you are using a chair instead of a seat. Having him put the toilet paper and contents of the potty chair into the toilet will remind him that, eventually, he will use the toilet because pee and poop belongs in the toilet. Rinse the potty chair out with water from the sink. Doing this after each time will help keep everything as clean and sanitary as possible. It will also reinforce with your child the importance of cleanliness in the bathroom. Once that is done, ask him to flush the toilet. Have him flush the toilet often to get him used to the sound the toilet makes and to create the habit of flushing. Doing this each time the doll goes pee or poop will allow him to practice these skills for when he needs to pee and poop. When he tells you the doll went pee-pee, celebrate with him, and tell the doll what a good job it did. Then wash your hands with your child and have him put a sticker on the doll's sticker chart. Repeat this process throughout the morning, alternating the fake pee with fake poop. Every couple of trips, do not put anything in the potty and tell your child that dolly must not have needed to go that time, but encourage him to congratulate the doll for staying dry.

At lunchtime, you will have a party to celebrate your child successfully potty training the doll. Give your child the gifts you wrapped the night before. A new potty storybook should be included in the gifts, possibly along with a short potty training video, and a package of big kid underwear. At this point, if your child still needs a nap to get through the day, you should have him take his nap. Otherwise, you can have him take off his diaper and put on a pair of the big kid underpants he just opened. Once he takes the diaper off, you should not put him in a diaper again.

The continued use of diapers

According to this method, once you take the diaper off your child, you should never revert to diapers. This is true even if you are going in public, visiting a friend's house, vacationing, or anything else.

To help prevent accidents in public, you constantly should be aware of where the bathrooms are and how much your child is eating or drinking. Continually ask your child is he needs to go to the potty. However, not all accidents can be prevented. Throughout the course of potty training and for a few months afterward, keep wipes and a change of clothes in your vehicle. This will enable you to deal with accidents wherever they happen. If your child pees his pants in a store and leaves a puddle, it is important to notify an employee so it can be cleaned up quickly, so no one slips and falls. Public accidents can be embarrassing for a parent, but it happens, and it is important not to overreact. You do not want to make your child feel embarrassed or ashamed. Remind him that accidents happen, and next time he feels he needs to go pee, he needs to tell you right away.

Allowing your child to wear a diaper after you have gone through a potty party will confuse him and cause increased accidents. This includes disposable training pants. Although some methods allow disposable training pants, this particular method views them as the same way as diapers. The only exception to the no-diaper rule is for nighttime sleeping. Bed-wetting is a separate issue from potty training, and children who wet the bed do so involuntarily. If your child is having problems wetting the bed, you should allow him to wear plain white diapers. Avoid pretty diapers with characters or pictures on them. Buy diapers that look as boring as possible, and tell your child they are "just in case" pants. He can wear them while he sleeps in case he has an accident in his sleep.

Once he puts on his new big kid underwear, take him to the bathroom and have him practice using the potty. During practice, he should pull his own underpants down, sit on the potty, wipe himself, drop the toilet paper into the toilet, flush the toilet, and then, wash his hands. Make sure you take the time to explain the different wiping strategies involved with pee 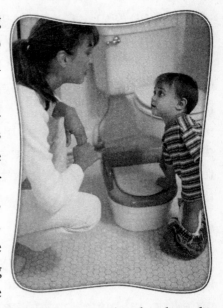 and poop, respectively. After he has practiced what he needs to do, tell him to let you know if he needs to go pee or poop in the potty. Take him back to the living room for some activities. Keep him drinking as much as possible. Every five to ten minutes, ask him if his underpants are still dry, and then ask him if he needs to go pee in the potty. You will do this until he tells you he needs to pee and does it for the first time. Once he successfully uses the potty once, congratulate him and have him put a sticker on his sticker chart. Then, remind him to tell you next time he needs to go pee or poop in the potty. Although at this point, you want to wait until he tells you he needs to go, watch for signs that he needs to go. If he starts crossing his legs, squirming, holding himself, or does any other physical action he typically does when he needs to pee, suggest to him that he should try to go pee in the potty.

Keep all the activities short, so he does not get too distracted. Distraction can lead to accidents. Continue offering him drinks throughout the day. The goal is that by dinnertime, he has used the potty several times. Depending on your child's natural bathroom schedule, he might not have pooped in the potty yet. This is OK. When you are aware of the fact your child needs to poop, either by the time of day it is or by the way your child is acting, gently lead him to the bathroom, and ask him if he needs to go poop in the potty.

At dinner, you will have a second celebration. This time, you will celebrate his potty training. You can make his favorite meal, have a couple more gifts for him, let him eat off a special plate, or you can take him somewhere special to eat, such as a favorite restaurant or relative's house. Encourage all other family members to make a big deal over his potty training and congratulate him for using the potty and being a big boy.

Possible activities for the potty party and potty party themes

Throughout the potty party, you should focus on short activities that allow plenty of potty breaks. In addition, you should try to keep conversations focused around the topic of using the potty correctly. Here are some ideas of possible potty party activities:

☆ Draw pictures of all the people he knows that use the potty.
☆ Play Simon Says.
☆ Charades
☆ Sing songs together.
☆ Make up new songs about using the potty that go to melodies he is already familiar with.
☆ Create a story with each other by taking turns making up a sentence.
☆ I Spy
☆ Read potty storybooks.
☆ Watch short potty videos for kids.
☆ Think up words that rhyme with words related to potty training.

These activities can go along with most potty party themes. Although a specific theme is not necessary for successful potty training, using a theme can help you focus the decorations, food, and activities. Here is a list of possible potty party themes. Choose one your child would get excited about.

☆ Magic theme
☆ Celebrity theme

☆ Circus theme
☆ Rodeo theme
☆ Your child's favorite super hero
☆ Rock star theme
☆ Farm theme
☆ Beach theme
☆ Medieval theme
☆ Cruise theme
☆ Traveling theme
☆ Your child's favorite cartoon character

CASE STUDY: POTTY PARTIES PUT INTO ACTION

Barb McCoy

CLASSIFIED CASE STUDIES™

directly from the experts

I had the hardest time potty training my son. I sought the advice of multiple people, I tried several different tactics, and I stressed over potty training for months. Finally, I went to a potty training class offered at my local library. The woman running the class was an expert on the potty party method of training. She suggested devoting an entire day to potty training but making it fun by having an all-day party. She made it sound so easy, so I figured it was worth a shot. My son was very into trains at the time, so I bought party plates and decorations to go along with a train theme. I also bought him a conductor hat and a teddy bear dressed as a conductor for the potty doll.

We spent the morning potty training the teddy bear. It went well, although I fumbled with the fake pee and made more of a mess than was necessary. I blamed it on the bear. We read a combination of potty training storybooks and train storybooks because I worried my son would get bored if we only read potty training books. He seemed to be enjoying himself and everything was going well. At lunch, we ate train-shaped peanut butter and jelly sandwiches. The gifts he received included a train whistle, big boy underwear, and the conductor hat. After lunch, I had him take his nap, which gave me a chance to relax. Despite having fun, the potty party was tiring for me.

After the nap, I had him put on his new big boy underpants. I did not have him put on regular pants because I figured it would be less to wash if he did have an accident. I set a timer for five minutes, and every five minutes we did a dryness test. When we did make trips to the bathroom, I had him wear the conductor hat, and we chugged like a train all the way to the bathroom. When he peed in the potty, I let him blow his new train whistle to celebrate. In between dryness checks we read more books, played a few games, and watched a train video. At the end of the day, we celebrated with his father and had all his favorite foods for dinner.

Although he stayed clean and dry for the day of the potty party, he did have a few accidents in the days that followed. Without me having him do a dryness check every five minutes, he did not always make it when he needed to. In response to this, I started watching the clock and regularly asked him if he needed to go. The good thing was that he did go when I asked him and he needed to. And gradually, over a week or so, the accidents mostly stopped, and he was reliably dry.

The days after the potty party

This method is referred to as the one-day method because by the end of the day, your child should be aware of how it feels to need to pee and what to do when he needs to pee. One of the most difficult parts of potty training is getting your child to tell you when he needs to go. This is not to say your child will not have any accidents after the potty party. In the days following the potty party, ask your child once an hour or so if he needs to go pee in the potty. If he is watching a movie or playing outside, suggest bathroom breaks. Watch for him to tell you when he needs to go. As you get more confident that he will tell you, you can stop asking him. If you are getting ready to leave the house, have him go pee before you leave. Take him to go potty about 15 minutes after drinking something. For example, if you go out to lunch and your son has a glass of milk with lunch, wait about 15 minutes before leaving and have him go to the bathroom beforehand.

Keeping track of what time your child uses the potty and whether he peed or pooped will help you know when to ask him if he needs to go. Often, accidents happen when the child is distracted playing or watching television, and the parents do not realize how long it has been since he last went potty. A time chart will help you keep track of your child's potty usage in the days following the potty party. The potty chart also will help you be aware of how many times a day your child uses the potty, and it will allow you to identify any sudden changes in his potty usage.

The chart on the following page is an example of a potty time chart. Just write either a one or a two in the appropriate box when your child uses the potty. You can create your own chart by adjusting the times according to the hours of the day your child is typically awake. If your child gets up before 7 a.m. or goes to bed after 9 p.m., you can adjust the chart accordingly. *This chart also can be found in the Appendix.*

	One	Two	Three	Four	Five	Six	Seven	Eight	Nine	Ten
7 a.m.										
8 a.m.										
9 a.m.										
10 a.m.										
11 a.m.										
Noon										
1 p.m.										
2 p.m.										
3 p.m.										
4 p.m.										
5 p.m.										
6 p.m.										
7 p.m.										
8 p.m.										
9 p.m.										

Pros and Cons

The benefits of this method are that it makes potty training fun, and if successful, the child will be potty trained in one day. The downsides to this method include the fact that there is still a certain amount of pressure on the parent to potty train the child successfully in one day. In addition, if the child is not fully potty trained by the end of the day, having a party to celebrate the success might be confusing to the child. This method also involves a lot of items and supplies that will add to the overall cost of potty training. A lot more preparation is needed to decorate and wrap gifts the night before. Finally, this method requires the child being potty trained to receive undivided attention. For parents with multiple children, this means arranging for the other children to be out of the house for the entire day. For many families, this might not be feasible.

Chapter 6

American Association of Pediatrics Method of Potty Training

The American Association of Pediatrics (AAP) set its recommended method of potty training based on its research regarding child development and readiness. The AAP is a strong supporter of a child-centered readiness approach and instructs parents to avoid potty training until the child is at least 2 two years old. Following this method, the child will set the pace for the potty training, and it is important for parents not to pressure their child or try to potty train her too quickly.

Overview of the Method

This method is designed to provide the child with an immediate reward for results. As soon as your child uses the potty, she gets a reward. Although the AAP does not dictate what appropriate rewards are, it does recommend stickers, and it discourages offering gradually larger rewards. There is a lot of support for the reward system of potty training. Dr. H. Patrick Stern, a developmental behavioral pediatrician, recommends providing the child with a small treat as a reward. He suggests that you keep the treats in a clear glass jar where the child can see them. This will provide the child with a constant visible reminder that she gets a treat if she uses the potty.

The foundation for the AAP-recommended method is waiting until the child is fully ready for potty training and demonstrates all or most of her designated signs of readiness. *These signs were discussed in Chapter 2.* The AAP recommends parents wait until their child demonstrates all or most of the stated signs. Although the AAP says children are likely to be ready to potty train starting at age 2, waiting for children to demonstrate most of the signs of readiness might require waiting until children are 2 ½, or possibly 3 years old.

By the time a child is old enough to demonstrate the signs of readiness, the child also will be old enough to reason with, which is why AAP recommends offering a reward. A child who is 2 to 3 years old is old enough to understand doing certain things will result in rewards. This method of potty training coincides with other methods of discipline the child already is accustomed to. At home or in day care, she has already experienced the reward of a treat for good behavior, so this method builds on that.

How to Prepare

You will need to demonstrate five primary factors for your child and practice them with your child. The first is your child's ability to pull her own pants up and down. By age 2, your child likely already is involved in dressing herself. This is particularly important before potty training. A child's inability to pull her own pants down and back up will lead to accidents, as well as a dependence on adults for assistance while using the potty. During potty training and in the days and weeks that follow, dressing your child in elastic-waist or loose-fitting pants is recommended. Being able to undress quickly will decrease accidents.

The second factor you will need to practice with your child is sitting on the potty chair. Often, children will not stay on the potty long enough to finish going to the bathroom. She either will stand up while still peeing or pooping, or she will need to pee and poop frequently because she is not going as much as she needs to each time. You can help her develop this skill by having her sit on the potty chair periodically while fully clothed. Have her sit there while you read a book or sing a song together. Doing this several times will get her used to the idea of sitting on the potty chair, and it will encourage her to sit on the potty seat for more than a few seconds.

The third factor is wiping. Wiping was discussed in Chapter 4, which is in agreement with what the AAP advises regarding how to wipe properly. To demonstrate and practice proper wiping, you can choose potty storybooks and potty training videos that effectively cover how to wipe. You also can have your child practice wiping in between diaper changes. Effective wiping is a skill that typically takes children years to master. However, it is important to provide your child with consistent reinforcement regarding proper wiping.

The fourth factor is flushing the toilet. Even if you have your child potty train on a potty chair as opposed to the toilet, your child still will need to learn how to flush and be comfortable doing so. Many children do not like the sound of a flushing toilet, and that discomfort leads to them not flushing regularly. Having your child in the room when you flush the toilet and allowing her to flush the toilet herself will help her flush the toilet on her own once she is potty training.

The final factor you will need to demonstrate and practice with your child before potty training is hand washing. As discussed in Chapter 4, hand washing is vitally important to reduce or eliminate the spread of germs. Proper hand washing involves using warm water and soap. Up to this point, you probably have washed your child's hands for her. However, it is important that she learns how to wash her hands on her own, as well as the importance of washing hands. You want to avoid your child only washing her hands when you are around to remind her.

Time to Potty Train

The AAP-recommended method of potty training follows four basic steps. No schedule or time limit is attached to these steps, and though parents typically hope to get through potty training quickly, the AAP asserts that potty training will take time. Unlike the choice offered to parents at the start of this book, the AAP recommends that once you put your child in regular underpants, you do not go back to diapers during the day. Consistency will be key throughout this method.

☆ **Stop wearing diapers.** The first step in potty training is taking your child out of diapers and dressing her in big kid underpants. It even recommends taking your child to the store and letting her pick out her own big kid underpants or buying underpants featuring her favorite cartoon character. Once your child stops wearing diapers, do not go back to them. Putting your child in regular underpants will help her feel like a big kid. Have your child wear clothes that are loose fitting and easy to remove during potty training. While at home during this time, you might choose to allow your child only to wear underpants. This will decrease the number of clothes you need to wash following an accident.

☆ **Watch for signs your child needs to use the potty.**
Getting your child to use the potty for the first time
is an important step in potty training. To do this,
you need to watch for signs that your child needs
to go. These signs might include crossing her legs,
holding her privates, dancing around, squirming in
a seat, turning red, or crouching down. Even when
children are accustomed to going in a diaper, they
still often show signs of needing to go immediately
before actually going. When you see your child
showing signs of needing to use the bathroom, gently
suggest she try to sit on the potty and lead her into
the bathroom. If your child is having trouble going
or is still not willing to sit on the potty long enough
to try, there are things you can do to encourage your
child. You can turn on the water at the sink faucet.
Often, the sound of running water makes individuals
need to pee right away. You can list all the people
she looks up to who use the potty; this can include
real and imaginary people. You can read her a book
or talk to her. Children often are more willing to sit
when they are getting a parent's undivided attention.
However, to avoid letting your child think sitting on
the potty is a means of spending time with mom or
dad, refrain from these tactics once your child has
used the potty at least once. Finally, you can try to
make her laugh by telling jokes or making funny
faces. Laughing will make your child relax and make
it easier for her to go potty.

☆ **Offer a reward for using the potty.** The reward for using the potty should be something small such as a small piece of candy or a sticker on a sticker chart. The reward also can be extra praise. Always keep the reward the same or on the same level; resist offering bigger rewards or extra rewards at any point. Gradually, as your child starts using the potty consistently, you will reduce and eliminate the rewards.

Treats, Not Bribes

One thing you want to be sure not to do is to bribe your child. There is a clear difference between giving your child a reward and giving your child a bribe. A reward is given after the child has done what she needed to do correctly, and a bribe is given on the promise your child will do what she is suppose to. For example, if your child goes all day without an accident, you can reward the child with a small treat. However, it is not good to give your child a treat at the beginning of the day and make her promise not to have an accident. This will not work for two primary reasons. First, they are called "accidents" because they are generally not intentional. Second, if the child receives her reward up front, there is no incentive for her to do what she is supposed to.

☆ **Use the early success to motivate.** Once your child has used the potty successfully once, you can use that as a means of motivation and a reminder of what behavior is expected. Continue reminding your child to try using the potty as you notice signs of readiness, but encourage your child to tell you when she feels she needs to pee or poop. Continue offering your child accolades each time she successfully uses the potty until she is staying dry consistently all day.

Pros and Cons

One pro of this method is that it is recommended by a trusted organization. The AAP bases its recommendations on proven research, and those making the recommendations are all reputable pediatricians. In addition, this method involves little to no pressure on the child. This is highly beneficial, particularly with children who tend to get stressed when under pressure. Children who react strongly to change likely will do well with a low-pressure method of potty training.

The downsides to this method include the acceptance of accidents and the lack of a timeline. According to this method, you are supposed to keep your child in big kid underpants but apply little to no pressure on the child actually to use the potty. This might lead to frequent accidents. However, the goal is to get the child to use the bathroom the first time quickly and then move forward from there. The AAP does not provide a timeline of how long this potty training method should take. It simply explains to parents that potty training is a process.

Chapter 7:
The Child-Temperament Method

T The child-temperament approach identifies the five basic child temperaments and tailors the potty training method to your child's temperament. This method takes the approach that because each child is uniquely different, one method cannot be applied to all children. The first step in using this approach is determining what temperament your child has. Once you determine your child's temperament, you can proceed with a method that is best suited for your child.

Tailoring the method to your child's temperament can avoid time-consuming setbacks because your child does not respond well to your potty training method. These methods use a number of different methods created and suggested by other potty training professionals. This particular approach, as a whole, is unique because it recommends specific methods based on your child. This method recognizes the fact that all children are different, and not every method is going to be successful for every child.

The Different Temperaments

There are five different temperaments that children might possess and that will affect their potty training. These five methods are sensory-orientated, internalizing, goal-directed, strong-willed, and impulsive. Each temperament has very features. However, most children will display qualities from multiple temperaments. It is important to choose the temperament you feel most describes your toddler.

Sensory-orientated: Sensory-orientated children are sensitive to loud noises, different tastes, and bad smells. They can get upset quickly and typically like to be comfortable. When potty training a sensory-orientated child it is important to keep the entire process calm and enjoyable. Sensory-orientated children will reject anything that makes them uncomfortable physically or emotionally.

Internalizing: A child who internalizes things will get frustrated easily if he does not experience immediate success. These children also will want to practice the new skills they have learned. It is important to celebrate the small victories with children who internalize. Small victories can include telling a parent he needs to go potty even if he does not make it to the bathroom or effectively pulling his pants down without needing any help.

Goal-directed: Children who are goal-directed will work hard when given a specific goal. They tend to be well focused and will be encouraged strongly by incentives and rewards for small achievements. For these children, accomplishing their intended goal is often reward enough; additional rewards are unneeded.

Strong-willed: Strong-willed children often are described as being stubborn. They will not do things if they feel they are being forced into it. For a strong-willed child to be potty trained, he needs to want to be potty trained. Strong-willed children tend to be emotional and might throw tantrums with little notice.

Impulsive: Impulsive children tend to be active and like to take risks. They are energetic and might get distracted easily, especially if they get bored. For an impulsive child, it is important to make potty training fun and interesting. If an impulsive child gets bored during the potty training process, he will abandon the effort and find something fun to do.

Discovering your child's personality

You can determine your child's temperament by analyzing his behaviors. The following lists of characteristics will help you identify your child's temperament. However, as you will notice, it might be difficult to target your child's exact temperament because most children display characteristics from each of these categories. If your child's temperament is not clear immediately based on the descriptions, read over the definitions again, and try to think about which temperament best describes your child.

Sensory-oriented

☆ Your child dislikes clothes that are scratchy or irritating in any way.

☆ Your child is easily scared by loud noises.

☆ Your child is uncomfortable in crowded places.

☆ Your child is a picky eater.

☆ Your child is sensitive to the temperature of water and likes to have his hands clean at all times.

Internalizing

☆ Your child never really tried to get into things he was not supposed to.

☆ Your child tends to want to stay with you all the time and will throw tantrums when separated.

☆ Your child seems extremely shy.

☆ Your child is easily afraid of things and tends to be afraid of trying new things.

☆ Your child tends to watch other children play rather than joining in.

☆ Your child gets upset easily and is difficult to console.

Goal-directed

☆ Your child can focus on one activity for an extended period.

☆ Your child is not easily distracted.

☆ Your child enjoys doing projects.

☆ Your child can follow directions and seems to enjoy being given directions.

☆ Your child enjoys doing things independently and enjoys showing off his projects when he is finished.

Strong-willed

☆ Your child is independent to the point he does not like people helping him.

☆ Your child can be stubborn.

☆ Your child tells people "no" a lot.

☆ Your child can get angry easily.

☆ Your child can throw tantrums for extended periods.

☆ The more you try to convince your child to do something, the more he resists.

Impulsive

☆ Your child has a short attention span when it comes to working on projects.

☆ Your child tends to be impatient.

☆ Your child needs constant sensory stimulation.

☆ Your child is physically active and enjoys trying new things.

☆ Your child has a difficult time sitting still.

☆ Your child seems to have endless amounts of energy.

☆ Your child makes friends easily.

How to Prepare

The first step to this method is determining your child's temperament type. To do this, read over the descriptions of each personality type in the previous section. Decide which description best fits your child's behavior and personality. Not all children fit into one personality type. It is possible that you will find your child demonstrates characteristics in two different personality types. If this is the case, read over the methods for each personality type and use the strongest points of each method. If you start with one method and realize it is not working, you can switch methods.

Based on the temperament approach you chose, read over the method description. Make sure any supplies you need are bought and prepared in advance. Regardless of the method you chose, it is important to be fully prepared once you initiate potty training. Be mentally prepared for accidents and minor setbacks. Each temperament approach will use a combination of universal strategies that have proven successful.

Universal Strategies

Universal strategies are common strategies that have been used in a variety of different methods. The temperament approach takes these universal strategies and recommends the strategies that work well with a temperament. Likewise, it recommends avoiding strategies that will not work well with a certain temperament.

This method uses seven universal strategies. Chose the strategies you are most comfortable with. Just because a certain strategy is recommended for a particular temperament does not mean you are required to use it. For example, if you and your other family members are not comfortable allowing your toddler in the bathroom while going potty, you can substitute role modeling with lots of potty storybooks and videos.

Role modeling

Role modeling is allowing your toddler to be in the bathroom with you and other family members while using the bathroom. This allows him to see what other people do in the bathroom, as well as the process of using the bathroom. Just as it is important for him to learn when he needs to pee or poop, he also needs to learn the process of going potty. Older children and adults may take aspects of the bathroom process for granted. Allowing a toddler to observe someone using the bathroom will teach him steps of the process you may forget to tell him verbally. For example, your son needs to learn to pull his pants down before he sits on the potty and not to stand up until he is completely done.

Positive reinforcement

Positive reinforcement is offering your toddler encouragement and accolades after each success. The temperament method encourages verbal positive reinforcement as to opposed to rewards such as treats or small gifts. Positive reinforcement lets your toddler know he did a good job, and he fulfilled your expectation. This praise will encourage him to repeat the same behaviors. Positive reinforcement also can be offered through stickers. Have a potty poster hanging outside the bathroom, and every time your toddler successfully uses the potty, he gets to put a sticker on the poster. The reward will be putting the sticker on the poster. This is different than a sticker chart, which uses stickers to track your toddler's progress toward a larger reward. Offering your child treats or small gifts can create a situation in which your child only will perform when he wants something.

Child's schedule

This universal strategy involves monitoring and recording your toddler's daily pee and poop schedule. Track the times of day your child pees and poops in his diaper. After a few days of this, you should be able to identify a pattern. If you are having a difficult time identifying when your child is peeing and pooping in his diaper, put him in washable training pants for a few days. Using rubber underpants over the washable training pants will reduce the potential mess of taking him out of diapers. Using washable underpants will make it significantly more obvious when he has peed or pooped. In addition, it will be uncomfortable for your son, so it will encourage him to start using the potty. Once you have an idea of his normal bathroom schedule, you can start bringing him to the potty at times of the day when he normally pees or poops.

Breaking down the process

Some children do not transition well during potty training. If your son is reluctant to start potty training or has anxiety about pooping in the potty, this strategy can be used. This strategy is separating peeing and pooping. Focus on teaching him to pee in the potty, and do not push him pooping in the potty until he has mastered peeing and he is comfortable with the process. This universal strategy can be applied with multiple temperaments. If your child is extremely resistant, you can break the process down even further and make sitting on the potty a step. Reward your toddler for agreeing to sit on the potty.

Props

The use of props can be used with every temperament type. The only difference is the type of props you use. Props include books, videos, dolls, and tracking sticker charts. Many toddlers respond positively to props because they make the process more fun. Books and videos can be borrowed from the library or from other parents. You can use dolls or stuffed animals you already own. Props do not need to involve additional expense.

Hop on the pot

This universal strategy is similar to the child's schedule strategy. However, instead of working with your child's schedule, you work with the daily schedule. Have him sit on the potty when he first wakes up, approximately ten minutes after he eats or drinks throughout the day, and right before bed. This will get him into the routine of using the potty, and it will involve times when he is likely to need to go. Create the opportunity for early successes will encourage your toddler to keeping working towards the goal of being potty trained.

Naked time

Naked time is exactly what it sounds: time your child spends naked. It is a successful universal strategy because it makes children immediately aware when they are peeing or pooping. This strategy will help your son know what it feels like right before he needs to go and when he starts going. This will solve the problem of him not realizing he needed to go until it was too late. Not all parents are comfortable with  naked time, especially if there are other family members living in the house or if you have frequent guests. If you do not want your child walking around naked, you can put him in regular underwear. The thinness of the material will make it immediately obvious when he has peed.

Time to Potty Train

If potty training is not immediately successful, refrain from assuming you chose the wrong method. Give your child time to adjust to the new experience. Only switch methods if your child seems confused or uninterested in the methods you are employing. You also may modify the chosen method slightly if you feel one of the other universal strategies will be more successful than the ones you are already using. You may employ additional tactics depending on your child's temperament. For example, as mentioned, goal-orientated children are driven. Choose an activity you know your child wants to be involved in and take him to observe the activity. While you are there, point out that none of the kids there are wearing diapers. When you are leaving, tell him that he can get involved in the activity as soon as he is done wearing diapers.

Sensory-orientated child

As mentioned earlier, sensory-orientated children are sensitive to touch, taste, smell, sound, and sight. Sensory-orientated children tend to be more difficult to train because they are less likely to adjust to things such as the coldness of a toilet seat, the difference in feel between diapers and underwear, the smell of a public restroom, and the sound of the toilet flushing. It is important to ease sensory-orientated children into these new sensory experiences.

The best way to do this is to practice with him before initiating potty training. Have him sit on the toilet a few times with his clothes on, so he can get used to how it will feel. Then have him sit on the toilet a few times without his clothes on, so he can adjust to the temperature of the toilet seat and the feel of the seat on his bare legs and bottom. Have him in the bathroom with you when you flush the toilet, so he can adjust to the sound of the toilet flushing.

If your child fights wearing underwear instead of his diaper, you can make it a slow transition. Have him wear underwear under his diaper, so he can get used to the feel of the fabric against his skin but still have the padding and comfort of a diaper. Each day fasten his diaper a little looser, so the diaper becomes uncomfortable for him to wear. Eventually, the diaper will be so loose that it will interfere with his play. By this time, he will have adjusted to the feel of the underwear.

With a sensory-orientated child, the two most helpful universal strategies you can use are role modeling and naked time. As mentioned, it is important to ease your child into the potty training process. Role modeling for weeks or even months leading up to potty training will give your toddler plenty of time to accept the training and to know what to expect when using the potty. Naked time will help him to know when he needs to use the potty without putting him in a situation where he is likely to wet or soil his underwear. Sensory-orientated children are likely to get upset after accidents. He will want to be immediately changed. The downside to naked time is if the air temperature is not suitable for your toddler, he may refuse to be naked. If your son is resisting the transition, you can then use the breaking-down-the-process strategy by only focusing on getting him to pee in the potty.

Internalizing

If your son has an internalizing temperament, then he is likely to take failures and accomplishments personally. He will take great pride in himself when he does something well, but he also can be derailed by a failure. Due to this, it is important to minimize failures and maximize successes. You can do this by celebrating small successes and by setting up the opportunity for frequent successes. Use positive reinforcement to celebrate every step your son takes in the right direction. For example, provide positive reinforcement when he sits on the potty, even if he does not go pee or poop. This will encourage him to continue sitting on the potty when you ask him to.

Use either the child's schedule strategy or the hop-on-the-pot strategy to get your child to sit on the potty at a time when he is likely to need to pee or poop. This will make it easier to get him to pee or poop on the potty early on in the potty training process. You then will use positive reinforcement to encourage the behavior. Internalizing children take great pride in themselves. In order to feel more accomplished, your son will make the effort to go in the potty each time he is aware of the fact he needs to pee or poop.

If your toddler still has frequent accidents despite his great desire to use the potty, let him have some naked time. It is possible he is not realizing the feeling of needing to pee or poop. In order to prevent him from being completely discouraged by accidents, downplay them as much as possible. If he has an accident, clean it up quickly and reassure him that it was just an accident, and everyone has them when they are starting out.

Goal-directed

Goal-directed children naturally are inclined to work toward a given goal. Although you want to give your toddler plenty of time, providing a deadline will help motivate him. This deadline can be the start of a new sport, a vacation, or preschool. Choose something he is looking forward to. Create a sticker chart to track his progress. Goal-directed children will enjoy monitoring their progress. Use positive reinforcement to encourage him to continue working toward his goal.

Learning your child's schedule and directing him to the bathroom at times he is likely to need to go will jumpstart his success and encourage him to keep moving forward. Similarly to the other temperaments, goal-directed children will learn through role modeling and the use of props such as books, videos, and dolls. Once he is reliably clean and dry throughout the day, congratulate him for accomplishing his goal.

CASE STUDY: POTTY TRAINING A GOAL-DIRECTED CHILD

Jeremy Parsons

I have one son. We decided to potty train him when he was two years old. We started out with a potty chair, but he really did not seem to like the potty chair, so we soon switched to the toilet. He responded well to this and quickly understood when and how to pee in the toilet. We did have problems getting him to poop in the toilet. When he needed to poop, instead of saying something or going into the bathroom, he would hide in a corner or behind the furniture and go in his pants. Even as a toddler, my son was very goal-driven, so we bought him some big kid underwear as an enticement to stop pooping in his pants. We told him repeatedly that it was very important for him to tell me when he needed to poop. The introduction of the big boy underwear worked, and he was completely potty trained by the time he was three years old.

Strong-willed

A strong-willed child can be the most difficult to deal with at times because strong-willed children need to feel in control. For that reason, it is important to create a situation where your child wants to be potty trained. Trying to force or intimidate your child into going potty will only strengthen your child's resolve to not use the potty. It is important not to try to use the child's schedule or hop on the pot strategies with a strong-willed child. These strategies put you in charge of when your toddler goes potty.

Universal strategies that work well with a strong-willed child include the use of props, positive reinforcement, and role modeling. Instead of initiating potty training, start role modeling and using potty storybooks and videos. You want to create a situation where your child will think it was his idea to start using the potty. When he makes steps toward using the potty, congratulate him. Positive reinforcement will encourage him to keep moving toward using the potty. However, be careful not to get too excited when he uses the potty. If he thinks you want him to use the potty too much, he may stop in order to maintain control over the situation.

Another way to encourage a strong-willed child is to create a sense of competition. Do not create competition with specific children your child is friends with or related to. Instead, point out kids at the park that are not wearing diapers, and tell your son you bet he can start going without diapers like that other child. You also can take him to the store and let him pick out his own underpants. Once again, as a means of maintaining control, your son may refuse to wear underpants you buy without him.

CASE STUDY: GIVING A STRONG-WILLED CHILD OPTIONS

Sara Andress

I had a hard time potty training my daughter. She is a strong-willed child, to say the least. She likes things to be her way and her idea. When she decided she did not want to use the potty, it was like repeatedly driving into a brick wall. I would make her sit on the potty for as long as I could, and she would not go. Then, when she got off the potty, she would almost immediately pee in her pants. She would then tell me she needed to be changed. I tried sticker charts and treats. She quickly adapted to this tactic and would only pee in the potty when she wanted a treat. The harder I pushed her, the harder she pushed back. For months I tried to force her to use the potty and stop going in her pants with no success. Finally, I gave up. I put her back in diapers and did not bring up using the potty for a few weeks. I had been advised to do this. However, the person giving me the advice told me that if I did not bring it up then she would start using the potty on her own. That did not happen.

Although we still had several months to go, I was starting to get worried she would not be potty trained in enough time to start preschool. In other areas of life, I had found that giving her options to choose from resulted in a more pleasant outcome, so I decided to apply that to this situation. I told her if she stopped wearing diapers, she could go to preschool. She said she wanted to go to preschool, so I said again that she could only go to preschool if she stopped wearing diapers. She verbally agreed, so I took her diaper off and let her pick out a pair of big girl underpants. After that, I periodically reminded her, but she started using the potty regularly. By the time preschool started, she was reliably dry, and I did not even feel the need to remind her to use the potty throughout the day.

Impulsive

Impulsive children can be more difficult to potty train because they are so active. Impulsive children are often so scattered that they do not easily recognize the need to go to the potty until it is too late. Naked time is an important strategy to use to teach your toddler what it feels like to need to go pee or poop. Use role modeling and props to teach your toddler how to use the potty to pee and poop. Breaking down the process will not be an effective strategy for impulsive children.

You likely will need to use the child's schedule strategy. Your toddler will be unlikely to stop what he is doing to go potty. However, if you stop him and take him to the potty on a regular schedule, he will take the opportunity to go. The key to this being successful is letting him go back to what he was doing before the potty break. If he starts to feel the potty break is used to get him to stop what he is doing, he will resist potty breaks. You also will need to take him to the potty when out in public. The key to long-term success will be keeping him on a potty schedule until he starts initiating potty breaks.

Pros and Cons

One of the benefits of this approach is that each method uses the same basic supplies, so there will be no need to spend additional money based on your child's temperament. The downfall to this method is that you likely would need to learn and follow a different method for each of your children. In addition, there is not a strong research base to suggest that children of different temperaments need different potty training methods. Finally, your child might not fit perfectly into one temperament type. Many children display characteristics of multiple temperaments, which might make it difficult to follow a temperament-based approach.

Chapter 8:
Stress-Free Methods of Potty Training

T he following methods are considered stress-free because they are relaxed approaches to potty training. Although the one-day method and the early potty training methods require parents to be vigilant about constantly keeping their child focused on using the potty, these methods stress putting absolutely no pressure on your child. Some of these methods could even be considered part-time potty training. Unlike most other methods of potty training, these methods do not require parents to stop using diapers as soon as potty training is initiated. These methods might be ideal for some parents who work a lot and are only with their children a few hours a day or parents who are already living with a great deal of stress. Children quickly and easily notice their parents' stress levels and will be stressed themselves. Taking a relaxed approach to potty training will provide an opportunity for potty training while not increasing the amount of stress already in the child's life. The downside to these methods is that they take a long time. Potty training using these methods will take months. However, according to the research supporting these methods, including research by Dr. Brazelton and Dr. Spock, potty training should be gradual and take more time.

The Basis for all Stress-Free Methods

Although there are multiple approaches to potty training that are considered stress-free, they all have the same basic principles. The first is that parents have to remain patient and relaxed the entire time. Parents should not push their toddler to use the potty or to sit in the bathroom. Parents need to respect their child's feelings about the transition from the diaper to the potty and respond according. These methods are not designed to happen in one day or one weekend. They are gradual methods that do not force toddlers out of diapers in one swift act. Although there are many benefits to potty training for children, they are not yet aware of those benefits, and taking the diaper away might cause anxiety.

Stress-free methods of potty training are also dependent on the signs of readiness recommended by the AAP. The group does not recommend attempting early potty training, and stress-free methods hold to the belief that children younger than 2 years of age are unable to understand potty training and are physically unable to control themselves. Dr. Spock's method of potty training and the Brazelton Method are both considered stress-free methods of potty training. These men, who were pioneers in the movement toward child-centered potty training, each developed stress-free methods, which they encouraged parents to follow.

Dr. Spock's method

Dr. Spock asserts that parents wait until a child is ready to be potty trained, which typically occurs between 2 and 2 ½ years old. Waiting until the child is ready will enable parents to potty train without forcing the child to do anything. Dr. Spock believes children will have better control over their bowels and bladders and will be willing and able to use the potty. To prepare your child for potty training, let your child be in the bathroom while other family members are using the toilet. Explain to your child that going to the bathroom is completely natural and normal. This will help children get past any fear or embarrassment they may feel regarding the potty. Avoid referring to pee or poop as gross, icky, smelly, or any other negative adjective. It is important that your toddler understands there is nothing wrong with pee or poop. Start teaching your child to wash her hands at an early age.

All you will need to follow this method is a child-size potty chair or potty seat, a step stool for hand washing, and books or toys to entertain your child while on the potty. Start by having your child sit on the potty chair fully clothed to get used to it. Because Dr. Spock recommends waiting until your child is older than

2, your child likely already will be able to pull her pants down by herself. However, if she still has trouble with this, have her practice pulling her pants down as well. Once your child is used to sitting on the potty chair, suggest she pull her pants down by herself and try to poop while sitting on the chair. At any point, if your child wants to get up or leave the bathroom, do not stop her. Doing so will make your child think she is being punished. Likewise, do not insist or pressure your child into going pee or poop on the potty. Let her dictate the process.

After you have gotten your child to sit successfully on the potty and pee or poop in the potty, take her to the potty two or three times each day when she is showing signs she needs to pee or poop. If you go in the bathroom and your child's diaper is still dry, praise her for staying dry. However, do not offer too much praise. Children at this age do not always like to be compliant, and too much praise might have an adverse affect. If she seems eager to use the potty, put the potty chair in an obvious location (if you are using one), take her diaper off, and tell her she can use the potty whenever she wants. If she refuses to use the potty or has an accident, put her diaper back on. Repeat this several times until she demonstrates control over her bladder by holding her pee in until she reaches the potty chair. Once she can do this, you can switch her diapers to training pants.

The Brazelton method

This method was created by Dr. Brazelton and is based on his research. Similar to Dr. Spock's method, the Brazelton method is based solely on the child's willingness and cooperation. The Brazelton method is based on five steps, and parents are instructed to stay on each step for as long as it takes the child to be completely comfortable and cooperating. If at any point your child shows resistance to a step, you are to go back to the previous step immediately and wait for your child to show signs she is ready to move forward again. This moving back might happen several times. It also might bring you back to the beginning. If your child resists a new step and then continues to resist even when you move her back a step, you might need to stop potty training and start over again.

Brazelton stresses the importance of not potty training until your child is completely ready. Although most methods focus on what signs of readiness to look for, Dr. Brazelton offers a list of signs that show your child is *not* ready for potty training.

☆ If she stands by the potty chair or toilet but then pees or poops on the floor
☆ If she fights you when you try to take her diaper off
☆ If she takes her diaper off and then poops on the floor
☆ If she does not appear uncomfortable when she clearly has poop in her diaper
☆ If she hides while pooping

☆ If she refuses or denies it when a parent asks if she is pooping or needs to poop

☆ If she shows any resistance to the potty chair or potty seat

If you child is demonstrating any of these things, Dr. Brazelton recommends you hold off on potty training and wait for your child to initiate an interest in potty training or a discomfort in going in a diaper. Once you think your child is ready to get started, you can start with step one.

Step One: Take your child to the store and let her pick out her own potty chair or potty seat. If she gets to pick it out herself, she will genuinely feel it is hers. Explain to her that she will have her own potty just like mommy and daddy have their own potty. This means buying a new potty chair or potty seat for each child you potty train, which will increase the overall cost of potty training.

Step Two: Let your child sit on the potty fully clothed. Sit in the bathroom with her and talk, sing songs, or read books. Do anything that might encourage your child to continue sitting on the potty. If at any point your child gets up or wants to leave the bathroom, let her. Never force your child to sit on the potty or stay in the bathroom for a certain period. Similarly to Dr. Spock's method, Dr. Brazelton stresses the importance of making sure your toddler does not feel punished or trapped in the bathroom.

Step Three: After your child is willing and comfortable sitting on the potty regularly throughout the day, you can start working on making the connection between the potty and the child's pee and poop. When changing your child, take the diaper and dump the contents of the diaper into the potty. Tell your child that poop and pee belong in the potty. If your child gets upset or mad at your actions, immediately stop doing it and go back to just sitting on the potty chair fully clothed. However, if your child accepts the new change, do it several times throughout the day. Ideally, at this point your child will take it a step further and start letting you know when it is time to empty her diaper into the potty.

Step Four: Take off her clothes and allow her to play and run around with no diaper on. If you have a yard and you are comfortable with your child being undressed outside, you can bring the potty chair outside for this step. Potty training outside will eliminate the need to clean up accidents in the house. Ask your child if you can help her go potty or if she can do it by herself. Follow her directives on whether she wants help. When she does go pee or poop in the potty chair, tell her she did a good job but, with this method, avoid getting overly excited. This will interfere with your child's chance to be proud of herself, and it might deter her from wanting to use the potty chair.

Step Five: At this point in the potty training, you can start using disposable training pants or washable training pants with plastic covers. This will allow your child to use the potty when necessary, but they will contain any accidents. Continue using training pants until she can go all day dependably without peeing or pooping in her training pants. If at first your toddler rejects the training pants, go back to diapers and follow Step Four for a few days or weeks. Then, suggest she try wearing the training pants again, and act according to her response.

Other stress-free methods

Although the two stress-free training methods described above were designed and promoted by reputable medical professionals, you might choose to use other stress-free methods. These other methods include simple rewards, gradual potty training, and a potty doll. Although simple rewards and potty dolls also are used in other methods, the stress-free approach to their use is different. Once again, these methods are not meant to work quickly; they are meant to work at the child's pace. The underlying principle of all these methods is to work at your toddler's pace.

Simple rewards

The simple rewards method is designed to let your child decide when she wants to use the bathroom and reward her for her initiative. Move your child from diapers to disposable training pants. Once a day, demonstrate for her how she is supposed to use the potty by either bringing her in the bathroom when you need to go or by having her practice sitting on the potty chair or seat. Then, tell her she can use the potty to go pee or poop whenever she wants. Throughout the day, you can ask her occasionally if she needs or wants to go pee in the potty. If she says yes, you can take her to the bathroom. If she says no, let it go, and ask again later. Each time she decides to go sit on the potty she gets a small reward. She gets an additional reward when she actually goes pee or poop on the potty. Once she is regularly peeing and pooping on the potty, you can stop rewarding her for just sitting on the potty and only reward her when she pees or poops. The reward can be a sticker, a small treat, or even the opportunity to spend some alone time with mom or dad. The goal of this method is for her to be motivated by the rewards to want to use the potty regularly. Once she is dependably dry throughout the day, you can switch her from disposable training pants to big kid underpants.

Gradual potty training

Gradual potty training is ideal for parents who are not with their children most of the day and have day cares or caregivers who are unable or unwilling to potty train. With this method, you will need about 30 small gifts individually wrapped in brightly colored wrapping paper. The gifts should be small toys or trinkets similar in size and value to McDonald's toys. You can find items at the dollar store. Place all the wrapped items in a box, and tell your child it is the potty prize box.

You will introduce your child to the potty by having potty time each day. Start with a one-hour period. During this time, take your child's diaper off and either put regular underwear on her, or let her move around with nothing on her bottom. Ask her if she would like to use the potty. If she does, take her to the bathroom. Once in the bathroom, show her what she needs to do. Make sure, if she is wearing them that she can pull her underwear down and back up by herself. Have her sit on the potty chair and try to pee. If she does pee, you can help her wipe and then wash her hands. Then, let her pick a wrapped prize out of the potty prize box. If she does not pee, let her leave the bathroom when she wants to and try again later. If she refuses to use the bathroom, do not force her.

When your child has her first accident, she will be wet and uncomfortable. Do not make her feel embarrassed. Just get a rag to clean it up, and tell her the pee went on the floor because she was not wearing a diaper, and next time she needs to make the pee, she should go in the potty. Take her into the bathroom, clean her, and get her new underpants. When the potty session is over, put her back in a diaper, and tell her she can try again the next day. Have these potty sessions each day, but try to make them a little longer each day. The longer she is not wearing a diaper, the more opportunities she will have to use the potty.

The potty doll method

Potty dolls can be effective because they allow the child to learn while teaching. This is the method used in the one-day potty party method. However, the potty doll also can be used in a stress-free method. The potty doll should be used in conjunction with other stress-free methods to help reinforce what is being learned. Start out with two dolls, one for you and one for your child. Have your child imitate you with her doll as you teach your doll how to use the potty. Together, help your dolls use the potty several times throughout the day. The next day, have your child work on potty training her doll by herself. This will be particularly effective if your child really enjoys playing with dolls or stuffed animals and often humanizes them. Once your child has had the opportunity to potty train her doll, suggest she try using the potty like the doll did. At this point, you can add in the simple reward method, the gradual method, or both.

The potty doll also is used in other more intense methods, such as the one-day method of potty training. Under this method, you can work with the potty doll for several days, if necessary. This method is then combined with another stress-free method to make the transition from training the potty doll to training the child. Although the potty doll is not described as part of Dr. Spock's or Dr. Brazelton's methods, it still could be used as a pre-potty training method of preparing your toddler.

Pros and Cons

Stress-free methods are relaxed and allow parents to potty train when it is convenient for them. This might be ideal for working parents who might not have the time to dedicate an entire day or weekend to potty training. These methods also allow the children to dictate the pace of the potty training, and this is important for some parents. In addition, allowing for the continued use of diapers, even during potty training, will prevent the need to clean up messes in the house or deal with accidents in public. The disadvantages of these methods include the extended use of diapers. When using these methods, children are potty trained at older ages, and the potty training might take considerably longer. In addition, if you have a reluctant or resistant child, these methods might not be structured enough to effectively potty train.

Chapter 9:
Early Potty Training Methods

E Early potty training methods are aimed to train children younger than 2 years old. However, these methods are also varied based on the age of the child you are trying to potty train. Four basic methods are based on the age of your child. Infant potty training is for babies up to 6 months old. Then, there is early potty training for children 6 to 18 months old and for children 18 to 24 months old. Finally, there is (late) early potty training for children who are 2 years old. Although 2 is the age recommended in other methods, this method is still considered an early potty training method because it is not dependent on the recommended signs of readiness.

Infant Potty Training

Infant potty training has been supported by research going back to the 1920s. This research was based on the study of African tribes where babies are able to pee on demand by the time they are 4 to 5 months old. Infant potty training is the norm in indigenous cultures where diapers are not used and mothers virtually carry their babies with them everywhere. In these cultures, their mothers carry around babies in slings for a good part of the day. This helps to motivate the mothers to avoid getting peed or pooped on while going through their day.

Infant potty training is just as much about training the parents as it is training the baby. Because babies are completely dependent on their parents for care, they are not able to initiate using the potty. However, babies naturally do not like to be wet or soiled. Although you will be able to train your baby to respond to cues and pee and poop when cued, you will need to train yourself to be vigilant and constantly observant of your baby's behavior. It is important to be aware of how your child acts immediately before peeing or pooping. The best way to observe this behavior is by leaving your baby without a diaper as much as possible. Although this will lead to messes, it is the fastest way to start potty training.

What you will need

For this method, you will need a journal to track your baby's schedule and your progress. You also will need either a pee pot or a potty chair. Because your baby will not be sitting on his own, you will need to hold him over the container he will be peeing and pooping in. It might be easier and more convenient for you to use an old pot or bowl. Your baby will not be peeing or pooping a lot at this stage, so you do not need to 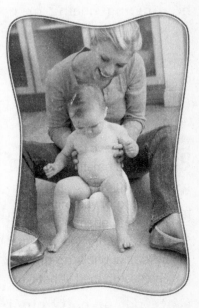 worry about him overflowing a pot or bowl. It might also be more convenient to have a pot or bowl designated for potty usage in each room where you will be with often your infant. This will allow you to get your infant somewhere quickly where it is acceptable to pee and poop.

How to prepare

Infant potty training has two parts. The first is learning not only your child's bathroom schedule but also his signs that he is about to pee or poop. The best way to learn these two things is by allowing your infant to go without a diaper as much as possible. This will allow you immediately to be aware of when your child is peeing. Keep a potty journal, and record what time of day your baby pees and poops and any observable behavior you noticed immediately before he starting peeing or pooping. Infants will display some sign immediately before peeing and pooping. This may be a facial expression, a change in breathing or skin color, or a change in temperament.

Potty training your infant

When you see your baby peeing or pooping, bring your face close to his ear and make either an "ssss" sound or a "shshsh" sound. Do this every time you see him going. After you are more aware of his bathroom schedule and his signs he is about to pee, start holding him over either a pee pot or potty chair when you believe he is about to pee or poop. As soon as he starts going, start making the "ssss" or "shshsh" sound in his ear and continue doing so the entire time he is going. After doing this for several days, you can proceed to having him go on command. When you know it is a time he generally goes, hold him over the pee pot or potty chair, and then, start making the "ssss" or "shshsh" sound in his ear. If the process has worked, he will start peeing when he hears that sound. The objective is to have him associate the noise with the action of peeing and pooping.

Baby Potty Training

The second level of early training is baby potty training, and it is targeted at children who are between 6 months and 18 months old. Potty training a child when he learns to sit

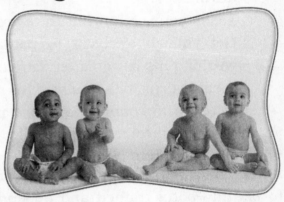

up decreases the need for you to hold your baby over a pot or potty chair. You can teach him to sit on a potty chair before and during potty training. Potty training at this age often works well because he is old enough to respond to parents' words and reactions, and babies this young have not yet hit an age of active resistance. Potty training at this age also provides many benefits for your child, including an early learning experience. Research on early potty training has shown that children who are potty trained at a younger age will finish potty training faster than children potty trained after the age of 2. Although infant potty training is based on getting your infant to respond physically to a verbal cue, baby potty training is designed to teach your baby how to use the potty. You will seek to accomplish seven goals during baby potty training.

☆ Get your baby to be comfortable sitting on the potty chair.
☆ Teach your child to pee and poop in the potty chair as opposed to the diaper.

☆ Allow your baby to exercise the muscles used during peeing.

☆ Teach your child what the word *potty* means.

☆ Get your baby used to potty routines, including washing his hands after each trip to the potty.

☆ Include trips to the potty in his normal daily routines.

☆ Get him to communicate his need to use the potty before an accident.

Although there is no set amount of time it takes for a child to be fully potty trained and dependably dry throughout the day, research shows that the younger your child is when you start potty training, the less time it takes to complete potty training. Even if infant potty training takes six months, if you started at 4 months old, your baby will be potty trained before his first birthday.

Preparing for potty training

For this method, all you need is a potty chair and a positive attitude. Before initiating potty training with your baby, place the potty chair in an area where your child can see it regularly throughout the day. This might be in a playroom, living room, or the baby's bedroom. Let your baby explore the potty chair, climb on it, sit on it, and grow accustomed to it being a part of his world. Encourage your child to play with the potty. Although most potty training methods discourage allowing your child to play with the potty chair, early potty training involves children who have yet to develop their verbal skills, so playing with the potty is encouraged in place of being able to explain to your child what the potty chair is for. However, you should direct the play toward things that will help reinforce potty training. For example, you can give him a doll or stuffed animal and tell him to have the toy sit on the potty. Finally, have your baby sit on the potty chair fully clothed while you read a book or play a game.

Potty training

Watch for signs your child is about to pee or poop in his diaper. Tell him he needs to go potty and repeat the word "potty" several times. Then, take him to the potty chair, take his diaper off, and sit him on the potty. You want your child to connect what he is doing with the word "potty." Any time you know your baby is peeing, either in his diaper or in the potty, repeatedly tell him, "You are peeing." Likewise, when he is pooping, tell him, "You are pooping." Similarly to repeating the word "potty" when he needs to go, this will enable him to connect the words with the action.

At this age, your child will not be ready to tell you when he needs to pee or poop, so it is important to take him to the potty at regular intervals to give him the opportunity to go pee or poop in the potty. Keeping him on a regular eating and drinking schedule also will make it easier because he likely will be peeing and pooping on regular intervals as well. Children who eat continuously or graze throughout the day are more likely to have an irregular bathroom schedule. Each time your baby pees or poops while sitting on the potty, you need to celebrate. Babies at this age respond well to positive reactions from parents. It is important to smile, laugh, and tell him he did a great job. The more excited you are, the more excited your baby will be to repeat the actions. If you sit your baby on the potty and he does not go pee or poop, do not say or do anything negative. Play with him so he sits there for a couple minutes, and if he has not gone, let him go back to his regular play area.

Although at first, you will be initiating the trips to the potty, your goal is to have your baby communicate to you when he needs to use the potty. To reach this point, you will need to teach your child what the word "potty" is referring to. To do this, place the potty chair either to the right or the left of your baby. Then tap on it with your finger to draw his attention towards the potty chair. When he looks over at the chair, get excited and praise him for looking at it. Then, walk him toward it, and have him put his hands on the potty chair. When he touches the potty chair, say the word "potty." Then have him sit on it. If you do this every time you have him try to pee or poop on the potty, he will soon associate the word "potty" with the actual potty chair.

The next step in teaching your child to initiate going to the potty is by getting him to crawl or walk toward the potty. Each time you want him to sit on the potty, move the potty a few feet away from him. Then, stand next to or behind the potty, so he can still see the potty chair, and call him toward you. Once he reaches the potty, praise him and have him sit on the potty chair. Each time you do this, you can move the potty chair a little farther away until he is crawling or walking completely across a room to get to the potty chair. This will teach him to go to the potty chair when he needs to use it.

Once he starts going to the potty chair when he needs to go potty, stop praising him for going to the chair, and only praise him if he actually goes pee or poop. This will turn the focus back to the ultimate goal of being fully potty trained. Continue praising him each time he goes pee or poop in the potty until he is fully potty trained and dependably dry all day. Although you should continue telling him he is doing a good job, you do not need to continue gushing over him each time. Also, even though he will be fully potty trained, he still will not be old enough to understand the importance of proper wiping and hand washing, so it is important to continue helping him with those tasks until he is an older toddler.

CASE STUDY: EARLY POTTY TRAINING

Dustin Parker

We have one son and one daughter. We decided to attempt potty training our children at a young age to save on the cost of diapers. We started by just letting them sit on the potty periodically throughout the day. We would encourage them to sit on the potty without their diapers on, and if they went pee or poop while sitting on the potty, we offered them praise. Even though we were taking an early potty training approach, we also took a relaxed approach to avoid resistance.

Both of the kids potty trained easily. We created a sticker chart for our son with progressive rewards. The more days he went without an accident, the closer he would get to a bigger reward, but there were small rewards along the way. Our goal was to give him small and large goals to work towards. Our daughter did catch on to it faster. She was going to the bathroom on her own by the time she was 18 months old. We still had a diaper on her to control accidents, but she would go into the bathroom, take her diaper off, and go pee in the potty. Although I have heard people say that girls potty train faster than boys, I am not sure if that was the reason behind the difference in our kids. Our son went through a significant family change while he was still a toddler, which may have interfered with the potty training process.

Toddler Potty Training

Toddler potty training is training children who are between 18 and 24 months old. By the time a toddler is this age, he is capable of physically controlling his pee,

and he will likely have some control over dressing and undressing. Children this age are also beginning talkers, so they will be able to communicate verbally the need to go potty. However, toddlers also tend to be more resistant to new things than babies are. You will need to convince your toddler to play along with your lessons while not encouraging resistance. You need to keep six goals in mind for yourself while potty training a toddler.

 ☆ **Control your own emotions.** It is important to teach your child to relax during potty training. Otherwise, he will have difficulty. The best way to teach your toddler to relax is to remain relaxed yourself. Being stressed or nagging your toddler to sit on the potty will have an adverse affect on the potty training process.

 ☆ **Be consistent.** Even after your toddler starts using the potty, it will take time before he will be able to communicate dependably to you each time he needs to go. This will be especially true if he is having fun playing or is otherwise distracted. To keep the progress moving forward and to avoid accidents, it is important to take him to the bathroom regularly. If you are unsure of his bathroom schedule, you can plan to take him to the potty 15 minutes after he drinks something, immediately after waking up, before going to bed, or every 90 minutes throughout the day.

☆ **Clean up accidents right away.** Although you should not reprimand your child for having an accident, it is important that your toddler understand what happened and what should have happened. If your child poops, scrape the poop into the potty chair, and tell your toddler the poop belongs in the potty. If your child pees, clean it up with a sponge, wring the sponge out into the potty chair, and tell your toddler the pee belongs in the potty.

☆ **Do not lose your temper.** Potty training can be frustrating at times, but it is important never to lose your temper with your child.

☆ **Reward all successes.** You should reward your child with hugs, smiles, and verbal encouragement. Because the process of potty training is sometimes slow, it is important to celebrate all success. For example, if your child sits on the potty for an entire potty session, reward him.

☆ **Enforce the potty rules.** Toddlers are at an age where parents can expect compliance during routines and activities. This applies to rules during playtime, mealtime, and now potty time. You will need to enforce certain rules and expectations during potty sessions Giving in to a tantrum will only prolong the potty training process.

Training sessions

You will have two goals during training sessions. The first goal will be to model how to use the potty, and the second goal will be to teach your child how to relax and sit in the bathroom. You should hold a training session once a day for approximately two weeks until you feel you have accomplished your two goals. For the training session, you will need a potty storybook to entertain your toddler, a book or magazine  for yourself, a timer, and your toddler's potty chair. To help you stay organized, you can keep all your needed items in the bathroom you are using for potty training.

Take your toddler into the bathroom, and close the door. Tell him he will need to stay in the bathroom with you until you go potty or until the timer goes off, then set the timer for ten minutes. Let him know he can either sit on the floor or sit on the potty chair and look at his book until you are finished. Then, sit on the toilet to go to the bathroom. If he tries to engage you in conversation, explain that you have to relax to go potty, and you cannot talk for a couple minutes. Once you start peeing, tell him you are peeing and ask him if he can hear the pee. When you are finished, ask him if he will get you the toilet paper. Once you get up, ask him to flush the toilet for you. Finally, wash your hands together. Try to stay in the bathroom for close to ten minutes. It is important during this time to not let your toddler leave the bathroom. He might resist at first, but after a couple of days, it will become routine. Continue the training sessions until he can remain comfortably in the bathroom with you for the entire ten minutes.

Potty training

The next step is to help your toddler make the connection between his own pee and poop and what you are doing in the bathroom during training sessions. Wait until he has pooped in his diaper. Then remove his diaper, and clean his bottom. Walk him into the bathroom and have him watch you scrap the poop out of the diaper into his potty chair. Tell him that his poop belongs in the potty. Leave it there for a moment and respond to anything he might say. It is common for toddlers to repeat what you just told them or to tell you that was their poop. After a moment, dump the poop from the potty chair to the toilet, and have him flush it. Then, you will set the timer and start a normal training session, except this time, encourage him to sit on the potty chair without his diaper on while you go potty. Drinking a lot of liquid throughout the day will help you need to go during these sessions. However, if you really do not need to go every time, that is OK. Go through the session like normal, but let him know you did not need to go this time. If he refuses to sit on the potty chair at this point, do not force him.

If you see he is about to pee or poop, tell him to hurry up and sit on the potty chair so the pee or poop goes where it belongs. If he refuses to sit on the potty chair, do not force him. After he has an accident, clean it up right away, and put it in his potty chair as described in Goal 3 of the toddler potty training section. Actually being able to see himself pee and seeing the puddle of pee on the floor will help him make the connection. Most toddlers have never seen themselves pee before because they are always wearing diapers. Repeat this process for several days until he goes while sitting on the potty chair. When this is accomplished, praise him for doing such a good job.

Once he starts peeing and pooping in the potty chair, you can stop the ten-minute potty sessions, but start taking him in the potty at regular intervals throughout the day. During these potty trips, you can sit in there with him and encourage him to sit on the potty and relax. Set the timer, as he already is accustomed to staying in the bathroom for ten minutes. If you are timing his bathroom trips right, he should need to pee or poop for all or most of these trips. At this age, do not rely on your toddler to tell you when he needs to use the bathroom. Continue following a potty schedule.

Potty Training Older Children

Although potty training older children is no longer considered early potty training, some experts suggest that using early potty training methods on older children is still successful. Using early potty training methods on older children has some advantages, as well as drawbacks. The advantages include the child's advanced social skills, verbal skills, motor skills, cognitive skills, and increased bladder size. These characteristics allow the child to understand what is happening better and decreases the number of required trips to the potty. However, early potty training methods require the parent and child to spend a significant amount of time in the bathroom. Older children are not always happy or able to sit in the bathroom waiting to pee. This can make the process frustrating for both the parents and the children. However, there are tactics that can increase the child's ability to relax while sitting on the potty.

One of the basic tenants of the early potty training methods is that the child sits in the bathroom until he needs to pee, as opposed to waiting until he needs to pee to go into the bathroom, as with many other methods. When you have reached a time of day when you are confident your child will need to pee, take him into the bathroom and have him sit on the potty chair until he goes. While he sits on the potty chair, you can sit on the regular toilet to keep him company and to make sure he stays where he is supposed to. If he is sitting there for more than 20 minutes and still has not peed, there is a chance he is too tense or restless to relax enough to pee. If this is the case, try playing relaxing music, tell him stories, or talk him through meditating. If he is really tense or stressed about using the potty, read him the book, *I Take a Deep Breath* by Sharon Penchina and Stuart Hoffman. This book teaches children how to relax through deep breathing. If you can get him to relax, his muscles will loosen, and if he needs to pee, he will be able to.

The goal is to have the child stay on the potty until he pees. Then, he will be able to see what he is doing. You can praise him for peeing, and when he is done, you can show him the pee in the potty. The goal is to make him aware of the physical feelings he had before peeing, the act of peeing, and what your expectations are. Once he is aware of these three things, you will be able to instruct him to go pee in the potty, and he will know what to do. This same method can be followed with getting him to poop in the potty. Although you want to stay in the bathroom until he goes, it is important to enter the bathroom when you think he needs to go. This will prevent him from having to sit in the bathroom for an extended period for no reason.

Chapter 10:
Dealing With a Reluctant Child

A A child might be reluctant to use the potty for a wide variety of reasons. Likewise, there are a variety of ways to deal with these issues. The first obstacle to overcome is finding out why your child does not want to use the potty. Since your child has limited verbal communication skills, it might be hard for her to tell you what is wrong. When dealing with a reluctant child, it is important to remain calm and positive throughout the process. Otherwise, you might worsen the situation by adding anxiety or stress to an already difficult situation.

Uncovering the Issue

The first thing you can do to try to uncover the issue is to talk with your child. Even with limited verbal skills, a child often can communicate a problem. Ask your child simple yes or no questions. For example, you can ask if she likes her new potty chair or if it hurts to go potty. If talking with your child does not help you understand, you should observe your child carefully to see if anything stands out. For example, you might notice your child does not poop regularly and often has smelly gas. This might be a sign your child is suffering from constipation or irritable bowel syndrome, which can make going to the bathroom painful. *Medical concerns will be discussed further in Chapter 12.*

Another possibility is that your child is experiencing emotional stress but is unable to understand her own feelings. Examine any changes she has experienced recently. This could be a large change like a move or the loss of a loved one, or it could be a relatively small change like a friend being moved out of her day care. She also could be reacting to parental stress. A parent's job loss or parents arguing can cause a toddler to feel stressed, and this will affect her potty training.

CASE STUDY: HANDLING UNEXPECTED ISSUES

Barb Stasiuk

I have two children, one boy and one girl. My son was almost three years old when he was completely potty trained, and my daughter was 20 months old. I first attempted to potty train my son when he was 28 months old. He was showing all the signs of readiness and seemed open to potty training. However, shortly after I introduced potty training, he came down with terrible stomach flu. The stomach flu experience was very traumatic for him, and after that, he refused to even go in the bathroom. He was so upset by the whole situation that I decided it was best to back off for the time being. I put him back in diapers, and we did not push using the bathroom for a while. Shortly before he turned three, I decided it was time to try again. Although I was sure he was ready, it was clear he had no interest in using the potty. He was content staying in diapers. I waited until I knew I would be home for a few days in a row. I bought big boy underpants, cloth training pants, and plastic pants. The night before I told him, "Tomorrow is the day you will not wear diapers anymore." He did not wear outside pants. At first, every hour and a half he would sit on the training seat. It was messy the first day, but then, by the third day he had only one accident and none after that.

With my daughter, she was very eager and willing to be potty trained. She was very interested in being a "big girl." One day when I went into the bathroom, she came with me and went on the small training seat. That is how I knew she was ready. After that, I bought her new "big girl" pants, and I started using the training pants with plastic pants. Within the week, she was potty trained. Overall, it was a positive experience. I was surprised by how quickly potty training happened once we committed to it.

The parent's perspective

Parents might be tempted to think their child is being defiant or refusing to use the bathroom intentionally. However, it is important to understand that moving from diapers to toilet training is a huge transition for a young child. It is often hard for children to understand their parents' expectations. Some children naturally do not respond well to change, and potty training might involve too many changes all at once. The best way to deal with a reluctant child is to remain calm and figure out what is causing the reluctance. The reluctance is the symptom of an underlying problem. Discovering and dealing with the underlying problem will deal effectively with the reluctance.

The child's perspective

Your child has spent her entire life so far wearing a diaper and has been able to pee or poop whenever she felt the need to do so. Potty training involves taking away her diaper and making her uncomfortable, possibly even embarrassed, when accidents happen. Potty training also requires her to become aware of and respond to feelings and sensations in her body that she has been allowed to ignore up to this point. She might not find the new underwear comfortable. Diapers provide extra padding between her private parts and her rough clothes. She might also feel cold being told to sit on a potty chair with no pants on. Your child might be scared of pooping, scared of the noise a toilet makes while flushing, or even scared to let her poop be flushed down the toilet. She knows she made it, and it came from her body, so she might be resistant to letting you flush it away. Your child might be feeling all these things during the potty training process. For a toddler, the easiest way to deal with unpleasant feelings or expectations is to refuse to cooperate.

To help your child get over the fear of pooping, start by reading her the book, *Everyone Poops* by Taro Gomi. This picture book helps children understand that pooping is perfectly normal, and everyone does it. It is important for children to know that pooping is not weird or gross or even dangerous. Ask your toddler what she is afraid of. Although young children are not always able to express themselves accurately verbally, sometimes they can. If she does express a fear that pooping will hurt, wait until she poops in her diaper, and then, point out to her that she did poop, and it did not hurt.

Resolving a compromised perspective

Some obstacles are easier to overcome than others, but all require a patient and positive approach. Children progress and potty train at different speeds, and even close siblings can pose drastically different obstacles. Avoid comparing children or feeling pressured by relatives or other parents. Focus on your child and your child's specific needs while potty training. If there are multiple problems, address one at a time. Keep the experience as stress-free as possible for you and your child. If the reluctance is due to emotional stress, spend time talking to your toddler about the recent changes she has experienced.

Most Common Obstacles and Their Solutions

Although this is not an exhaustive list, the following sections highlight some of the more common obstacles faced by parents and children trying to potty train. Some of these obstacles are simple to resolve, while others will require more time and patience. No matter what the obstacle is, there is a solution. Although there will be days you might feel your toddler will never be fully potty trained, keep reminding yourself she will be eventually.

Fear of the unknown

Using the potty is a change your child might be afraid to make. To lessen her fears, read her plenty of potty storybooks, watch potty training videos, and let her in the bathroom while other family members are going potty. If your child has a sibling, friend, or close relative who recently went through potty training, have that child assure your child that it is not scary. For many preschoolers, peer support is effective. Talk about the potty frequently, and talk about pee and poop while you are changing her diaper. The more you can normalize everything, the less afraid she will be to pee and poop in the potty. You also should ask her if she has any questions.

Lack of interest

Active children can be difficult to potty train because they do not want to stop what they are doing long enough to use the bathroom. Some active children get so involved in what they are doing that they do not even realize they need to use the potty until it is too late. Your child might not see the benefits of potty training and, therefore, will not want to interrupt her playtime to go use the potty. This is a common problem with both boys and girls and often is seen in impulsive children.

One way to deal with this is to schedule bathroom breaks. This will prevent your child from waiting too long to go to the potty. Another thing you should do is to let your child resume the same activity after using the bathroom. For example, if your child is playing outside, and you bring her inside for a bathroom break, let her go back outside after using the bathroom. If you use the bathroom as a means of getting your child to come in the house, your child will learn from that and refuse to come in the next time. Letting your child back outside for even a few minutes after the potty break will help make sure she does not connect bathroom breaks with not being allowed to resume play.

You also could try a potty training method that involves a reward. Present your child with an ultimate goal. For example, if your child loves baseball, you can tell her she can join the T-ball team once she is potty trained. Coordinating this goal with a sticker chart to track progress will give your child a solid reason to stop playtime to use the potty when necessary.

Make potty training more interesting by making it more fun. You can create a song or game for your child to play that involves going potty. For example, for little boys, you can buy a fireman's hat, and tell your son he has to pee in the potty to put out the imaginary fire. Then, let him wear the fireman's hat while he pees. For little girls, you can decorate the bathroom like a princess castle, or paint her toenails while she sits on the potty. To go along with the princess theme, have a princess crown in the bathroom that she only wears when she is sitting on the potty.

Parent not fully committed

If a parent is not fully committed to potty training, it might confuse the child. Although some methods are more passive than others, all of them require regular redirection to the potty. Parents who are not fully committed tend to be irregular in their potty training method. This will leave the child unsure of when she is supposed to go pee in the potty and when she is supposed to pee in her diaper.

The solution to this problem is simple: Get fully committed. Talk to all caregivers who spend regular time with your toddler. Discuss your chosen potty training method, and discuss your expectations and your goals for potty training. If you feel anyone is not supportive or fully committed, leave that person out of the process if possible. If that is not possible, then talk to your child about the home rules. Home rules will be the potty rules your child will follow while at your house. This tactic is particularly helpful when the child's parents do not live together.

Likes the convenience of going in a diaper

Although it is not pleasant, most kids are accustomed to the smell of their own poop. Most diapers are so well designed that the child does not feel wet after she has peed in the diaper. This overall lack of discomfort can lead to the child preferring to wear a diaper than be potty trained. Being potty trained means having to make regular bathroom breaks, which can interrupt playtime. To deal with this issue, you need to make it uncomfortable for your child to remain in diapers. The best way to do this is to switch to training underwear and plastic pants. The plastic pants cover will keep all or most of the mess contained, so you are not constantly cleaning up after her. However, the cloth training underwear will get wet and uncomfortable every time she pees or poops.

The Parent-Child War

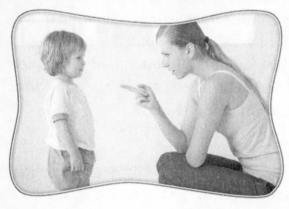

Another problem parents might face during potty training is a resistant child. This is when a child refuses to be potty trained as a means of maintaining control, as seen in the case study in Chapter 7. Toddlers are at an age where they are told what to eat, what to wear, what to play, when to eat, when to play, when to sleep, and so on. They have no control over their daily lives or schedules. Potty training is one area in which a toddler may realize she can assert control. This is especially true in situations when the parents have put too much pressure on the child to use the potty or have demonstrated for her that they desperately want her to use the potty. In this situation, losing your temper or getting emotional will only fuel her refusal to use the bathroom.

The best way to deal with a power struggle is to surrender power temporarily. Tell your child that you thought she was ready for potty training, but clearly, her body is not ready to use the potty. Let her know that it takes a big girl to use the potty, and she just is not ready yet. Then, take the potty chair and any other potty training supplies you have out of the bathroom, and put them away in a closet. Make sure your daughter sees you putting everything in the closet, and tell her you will bring everything back out when she is ready. Then, wait for about three weeks before bringing it up again. Do not mention potty training or talk about potty training, and inform other family members not to bring it up. There is a good chance that before three weeks are up, your toddler will bring up using the potty.

Overcoming a communication breakdown

Trouble communicating with your toddler about potty training can cause a frustrating situation that can lead to your toddler losing interest in potty training. A communication problem might be most evident when your child does not seem to understand when you want her to sit on the potty. If your toddler gets upset when she has an accident, yet frequently has them, it is likely she does not fully understand when she needs to go pee.

One of the best things to do when this happens is to slow down. The stress of being pushed toward potty training can be the underlying cause of your toddler's apprehension. Do not talk about potty training for a few days. If your child uses the potty, praise her, but if she has an accident, just let it go. After a couple of days, start reminding your daughter of all the people in her life that use the potty. Watch a potty training video together and reintroduce potty training storybooks. Naked time also might help her understand. Wait until she starts peeing, and then tell her what just happened. After the stress of the situation has subsided, and your child does not get agitated when you bring up the topic of using the potty, try it again using a stress-free method.

Assessing and Changing the Approach

Many of the potty training methods discussed in this book are vastly different. They use different signs of readiness, different approaches, and different rules. You likely will choose the method you feel will work best with your child and your lifestyle. However, that does not mean your child will respond positively to the method you choose. You might realize after some time that the method you chose is not going to work, and you will need to move in a different direction. The following section will provide a list of signs to look for. Avoid changing methods if your child is not demonstrating these signs. If potty training is not going as quickly or as easily as you thought it would, do not change methods. Changing methods often or without giving your toddler a chance might derail the potty training process and cause resistance from your toddler.

Knowing when it is time to use a different approach

Some signs your chosen method is not working are:

☆ Your child is highly resistant to the process.
☆ Your child still has regular accidents.

☆ Your child does not understand what she should be doing.

☆ Your child is getting stressed or frustrated easily.

☆ Your child hides the potty chair.

☆ Your child hides from you when she needs to use the potty.

When your child starts demonstrating any of these signs, you need to consider what is wrong with the approach you chose. Possibly, you are giving your child too much control, and your child needs more direction. It is also possible that the method you chose placed too much pressure on your child or too much emphasis on the need to potty train. If your child's days are filled with nothing but potty training exercises and discussion, your child is likely to get bored with it or want to avoid the situation.

Transitioning into a new approach

In order to start a new potty training method, you need to give your child a break from potty training. Allow her the opportunity to relax. Put your child back in diapers, but tell her she did not do anything wrong, and she is not being punished. Let her know that you think her body might not be ready to use the potty right now, and you can try again later. Then, take the potty chair out of the bathroom and put it in a closet or somewhere else that is out of sight. Wait three weeks without trying to get her to use the potty or talking about the potty training. Once three weeks have passed, start the new method you chose. When you start a new method, start with the preparation recommended for the new method. Do not try to build the new method on what you taught her with the old method. Start fresh as if it is your first attempt, and do not remind your child about the previously failed attempts.

Remain positive and encouraging

It has been stated repeatedly throughout the book that it is essential to stay positive and encouraging throughout the potty training process. This is particularly true when potty training after a failed attempt. Your child already will be sensitive due to the previous failure. It is important to be positive so your child does not feel embarrassed by the previous failure, and it is important to be encouraging, so your child does not think you expect her to fail again. With a positive and encouraging attitude, it is distinctly possible your child will respond favorably to the new potty training approach.

Use different terminology

It is also possible that a potty training attempt failed because your child did not fully understand the words you were using during potty training. It is important to make sure all caregivers are using the same terms and that your child understands each term. Your child should understand the term you decided to use for urine, stool, the toilet, the need to use the toilet, and his or her private parts. For example, if you are asking the child if she needs to go pee-pee and she does not know what pee-pee is, she will say no and then have an accident.

To make sure your child understands the terms you are using, you can ask your child specific questions. For example, after taking a diaper filled with poop off your child, ask her if she pooped. Then show her the diaper and ask her where the poop is. Ideally, she will point to the poop. If she does not, you need to work on teaching her what "poop" means. This applies regardless of the terms you decided to use. Likewise, you can ask your child to show you where the potty is. If your child cannot do that, you need to work more on helping her understand the terms you are using. This can be done through visual cues and repetition. Every time you take her into the bathroom, talk about using the potty, and point out the toilet paper and the toilet. Every time you change her diaper, tell her whether you find pee or poop in her diaper. Start showing her the diaper and asking her what is in the diaper. Doing this will help your daughter make the connection between the words and what they mean.

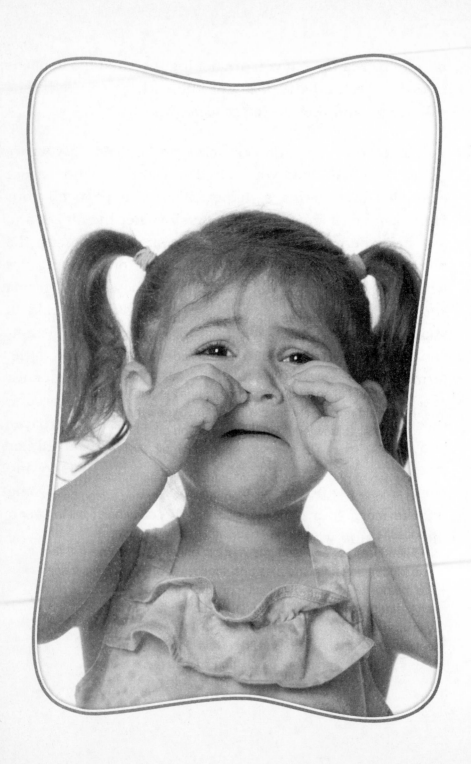

Chapter 11:
The Nighttime Bed-Wetting Issue

Bed-wetting means children pee in their sleep. Without a diaper on, this will result in the child, the bed linens, and the mattress getting soaked with urine. This creates an unhealthy sleeping environment for the child, as well as a cleanliness and odor issue. Although parents may be eager to deal with this issue, it is not always a simple problem to solve. According to the American Academy of Pediatrics, 5 percent of 10-year-olds still wet the bed. The best thing a parent can do is decrease the likelihood that the child will pee in his sleep, provide the child with comfort and support, and take measures to protect the mattress and room from the negative affects of the urine.

It is important for parents to keep in mind that bed-wetting is not a discipline or a training issue. If your child frequently wets the bed, it means he either lacks the physical ability to either go all night without needing to pee or the ability to wake up from the need to pee. Although some sources may suggest ways to "cure" or "solve" bed-wetting, it is important to understand it is something your toddler is unable to control. However, there are tactics you can follow to reduce the chances of bed-wetting and to minimize the situation.

Three physiological factors affect a child's ability to not wet the bed. First, his nervous system needs to be developed enough to wake him up when his bladder needs to be emptied. Second, he needs to have enough of an antidiuretic hormone called vasopressin in his system to slow urine production during the night. This typically develops when a child is between age 2 and 3. Finally, his bladder needs to be large enough to hold urine for several hours. Without these three factors, a child will not be able to control his bed-wetting.

Creating a Safe and Comfortable Environment

It is important to understand that children do not intentionally wet the bed. It happens while the child is sleeping, or the child may wake up while urinating but is unable to stop at that point. Bed-wetting is a problem that can cause a child to become extremely self-conscious and embarrassed. For these reasons, it is important to create a supportive environment for your child. Make sure he knows bed-wetting is not his fault and that you do not blame him. However, make sure he understands that you want to work with him to try to make it better.

Never criticize your child for wetting the bed or try to shame him into stopping by telling others he wets the bed. Allow your child to trust you with the information, so he can feel safe asking for help when he wakes up wet. Trying to clean everything up himself or hide the fact he has wet the bed will contribute to the spread of bacteria. In addition, you do not want him to feel marginalized at school. Although it is likely that he will not be the only child in his class who still wets the bed, he still might be made fun of openly if his classmates found out.

Setting up the bedroom

Make sure the room is clean, and it is easy to get around. If he does wake up during the night, he will need to get to the bathroom without any delays. If he shares a room with a sibling, he should either have his own bed or the bottom bunk of a bunk bed. Many times, a child will wake up but with very little warning that he needs to pee. This creates a situation where he will need to get himself to the bathroom quickly before having an accident. You can purchase a plastic mattress protector from a store that carries baby and toddler items. This will go on the mattress under the sheet to protect the mattress. When accidents do happen, you can change his sheets. The mattress cover can be cleaned using a spray disinfectant and paper towel.

Keep extra sheets in his bedroom closet. This will make the process quicker and easier so everyone can get back to sleep.

If possible, have him sleep in a room near the bathroom. If that is not possible, make sure the path from his room to the bathroom is an easy one. Obviously, some houses do not allow for having him sleep near the bathroom. If your son is waking up but not making it to the bathroom quickly enough, put a potty seat in his bedroom until he is able to make it to the bathroom. Making the bathroom as accessible as possible will help if your child is waking up at all. However, if he is not waking up, this will not make the situation any better.

Encouragement when bed-wetting occurs

Although the middle of the night is never the ideal time to have to clean up a mess or deal with a bathroom problem, avoid the temptation to get upset or frustrated. It is important for your child to know you support him and understand he is not doing it on purpose. When bed-wetting occurs, tell him everything is OK while you change his sheets and pajamas. Let him know you are not upset and that you understand it was an accident. Clean him quickly in the bathroom or keep baby wipes in his room to wipe the areas where the urine touched his skin. In the morning, have him bathe to avoid smelling like pee when he goes about his day. Do not remind him about the bed-wetting. If you do discuss it with him, continually remind him that it is not his fault.

When Can a Child Sleep without a Diaper?

Nighttime training should be dealt with separately from daytime training. Because nighttime training is so different, and you will not know right away if your child is going to have a bed-wetting issue, you do not want to have setbacks in daytime training because your child is upset over a nighttime accident. Throughout potty training, continue to have your child sleep wearing a diaper or disposable training pants. Pay attention in the mornings to whether his diaper is still dry. Make sure you have him try to use the potty right before bed and right after waking up.

If he is reliably dry when he wakes up each morning, then it is safe to try putting him to bed without a diaper after he is no longer wearing a diaper during the day. To be safe, you still should buy and use a mattress protector until you are confident he will not have nighttime accidents. It does not take much to ruin a mattress. When you stop putting him in a diaper at night, be sure to continue letting him go to the bathroom right before bed and right after waking up. Let him know if he wakes up during the night and needs to pee that it is OK for him to use the potty.

Put him in pajamas that he can easily remove to use the bathroom. Keep a baby monitor in his room, so you can hear if he wakes up to use the bathroom. Getting up and helping him during nighttime bathroom trips will help avoid accidents in places other than his bed. Some children are able to wake up when they need to pee, but they are not fully awake. This causes them to be confused easily and possibly pee in places other than the potty without realizing it.

Should your child stop wearing diapers at night?

Here are four signs your child is ready to stop wearing diapers at nighttime:

1. He suggests not wearing diapers to sleep in. Self-confidence is always a good sign during potty training.

2. He can "hold it" during the day. If he demonstrates he can hold it when he needs to go but is not near a bathroom, he can hold it at night.

3. If he wakes up regularly in the morning with a dry diaper, that means he is able to withhold the need to pee while sleeping.

4. If he wakes up during the night and tells you he needs to pee, you will know he is able to recognize the need to pee in his sleep.

Techniques to Prevent Bed-wetting

As explained earlier in this chapter, if a child is unable to hold his pee during the night and unable to wake up when he needs to pee, then the goal will be to prevent the need to pee during the night. Either way, the goal is to protect your child's self-esteem from the shame and embarrassment he might feel from frequent bed-wetting. You can do several things to achieve this. These techniques are not exclusive of each other, and you can employ multiple techniques simultaneously.

No drinking before bed

Stop allowing your child to drink liquids about one hour before bedtime. This will decrease the production of urine in your child's system during the night. Discourage him from getting up and drinking water during the night. Do not let him take a glass of water to bed with him. The more he drinks, the more he will need to pee during the night. If your child does wake up thirsty during the night, give him a small sip of water. If he drinks more than a sip, wait about 15 minutes, and then, wake him and have him try to pee in the potty. This is not the ideal situation, but it will be better than having another accident.

Encourage him to use the bathroom right before bed

Have him use the bathroom right before lying down to go to sleep. This will decrease the chance of his bladder filling during the night. One of the three physical reasons children wet the bed is that their bladders are not large enough to hold a lot of liquid. Sending him to bed with an empty bladder will decrease the likelihood of his bladder being able to fill during the night. Going to the bathroom right before bed is a habit most adults have as well. Point out to him that you also go to the bathroom right before bed, so he does not feel he is being treated differently. Trying to pee in the potty should become a part of his regular nightly routine.

Wear disposable underpants

A wide variety of nighttime disposable underwear is available for children who have issues with bed-wetting. Some companies, such as Huggies® and Pampers, make disposable underpants that visibly resemble regular underwear, so others will not know the child is wearing protective underpants. This will allow the child to avoid the embarrassment of being seen in a diaper.

Having your child wear disposable underpants only at night also will protect your child's clothes, bed linens, and mattress. It will allow everyone to sleep better because you will not be getting up to clean up an accident. Finally, it will relieve your child from the stress of worrying whether he will have an accident during the night. Although some potty training methods suggest that putting your child in a diaper once he is potty trained will derail potty training, there is a simple way to address this issue. Tell your son that if he wakes up and needs to go, he still needs to try to pee in the potty. Let him know the disposable underpants are there just in case he does not wake up.

Schedule nighttime bathroom breaks

If you regularly get up during the night to use the bathroom, then wake your child up, also. Have him go to the bathroom with you. If you typically do not go to bed for several hours after your child goes to bed, then get him up to use the bathroom right before you go to bed. If you need to, set an alarm for a set time during the night to wake up and take your son to the bathroom. Either way, it will allow your son the opportunity to empty his bladder during the night. As long as he does not pee before the bathroom break, this should prevent a bed-wetting accident.

Teach your child to use the bathroom during the night

If your child is waking up but having trouble making it to the bathroom, practice nighttime bathroom visits during the day. Have your child lie in bed and then get up and practice going through the process of using the bathroom without you giving him step-by-step instructions. The other option is to teach him to wake you up as soon as he realizes he needs to pee. That way, you can help him through the process and avoid the mess of an accident.

What Age Should a Child Stop Bed-wetting?

Every child develops at different speeds and different ages. There is no set age a child should stop wetting the bed. Some individuals experience bed-wetting issues into adulthood. Typically, bed-wetting stops before puberty. If your child is over the age of five and still regularly wetting the bed, it might be helpful to figure out the cause of the problem. If your child only occasionally wets the bed, it might be the result of a dream, fear, or other temporary cause. In these situations, help your child get cleaned up and change the bed linens, but downplay the situation to minimize the possible embarrassment your child may feel. One or more of the suggestions already addressed in this chapter may remedy the problem.

How long should a child stay in a training diaper to sleep?

The simple answer to this question is: as long as the child is wetting the bed. Taking a child out of nighttime training pants will not stop bed-wetting. It only will stop the containment of the problem. If you sincerely believe your child is waking up and choosing not to walk to the bathroom, taking away the training pants may be appropriate. However, you should still address the issue with your child. It is possible that your child is choosing not to go to the bathroom because he is afraid of the dark or of feeling alone in the house. If that is the case, instructing your child to call for you so you can walk him to the bathroom or leaving some lights on might solve the problem.

When to seek a doctor's help

Bed-wetting in and of itself is not a medical problem. However, you should see a doctor about bed-wetting in several situations. For example, if your child is still regularly wetting the bed after the age of five, you should bring it up with the child's doctor. At that point, you can assess whether there is a physical reason your child is wetting the bed. In some cases, bed-wetting is a symptom of a larger issue. Frequent bed-wetting can be a symptom of a urinary tract infection (UTI). *Chapter 12 will go into more detail about UTIs.* However, the symptoms of a UTI will be evident during the day as well. Bed-wetting is also a common symptom in cases of child sexual abuse. If your child was staying consistently dry during the night and then suddenly started wetting the bed on a regular basis again, you should bring it up to the child's doctor.

Chapter 12:
Common Medical Concerns

A wide variety of common medical issues can arise or become an obstacle during potty training. These easily treatable conditions may require taking the child to see a doctor. If you are concerned your child has a medical problem, the sooner you see a doctor, the better off the child will be. Sometimes these issues can interfere with your child's potty training by making your child afraid to use the potty. For example, if your child is constipated, pooping may be painful. If your child associates the pain with using the potty, he will resist pooping in the potty for fear it will hurt.

Urinary Tract Infections

A urinary tract infection (UTI) is a medical condition that more commonly affects females than males. However, in males, it is more common in uncircumcised males than circumcised males. A UTI can range from painful and annoying to very serious. It is always important to take your child to the doctor if she shows signs of a UTI. Common UTI symptoms are:

☆ Persistent need to pee
☆ Burning sensation while peeing
☆ Peeing frequently, but in small amounts
☆ Pee appearing cloudy
☆ Pee that looks pink or dark brown
☆ Strong-smelling pee
☆ Pelvic pain in girls
☆ Rectal pain in boys

If your child demonstrates one or more of these symptoms, you should take your child to see the doctor. Your child's doctor can prescribe a medication specifically designed to deal with UTIs.

The urinary system is composed of the urethra, bladder, ureter, and kidneys. A UTI is an infection in any of these body parts. Although a UTI in the kidneys is possible, UTIs in the bladder and urethra are more common. UTIs are common in young girls and can be caused by a couple of things, including improper wiping. UTIs are treatable with medication, which is one reason it is important to see a doctor if a UTI is suspected. If left untreated, a UTI can lead to acute or chronic kidney infections that can permanently damage the kidneys.

How to prevent UTIs

Two of the most common causes of UTIs in young girls are improper wiping and too many bubble baths. If your child is wiping from back to front, she likely is smearing fecal matter. This easily can cause a UTI. It is very important to teach your little girl how to wipe properly and to help her wipe until you are confident she can do it herself. The other common cause of UTIs in little girls is bubble baths. When a little girl sits in a bubble bath, she is being exposed constantly to the bubble bath soap. Frequent exposure can lead to an infection. Bubble baths should be limited to once a week; fewer if your daughter seems to develop UTIs quickly. In addition, have your child drink lots of water. Water will help to flush out any bacteria that make their way into the urinary system. Cranberry juice also has been found to be helpful in preventing UTIs.

Constipation

Constipation is a common gastrointestinal problem in both adults and young children. Constipation is classified as either infrequent bowel movements or difficulty passing a bowel movement. Constipation can cause poop to be hard and painful to pass. Although not all children will normally poop every day, that does not necessarily mean they are constipated. Constipation should be considered as a problem if your toddler is pooping fewer than four times a week, and the poop is hard. Constipation can result in your child avoiding pooping. However, this will only make the constipation worse.

Constipation occurs when the food waste is not moved through your toddler's intestines fast enough. This can be caused by a number of things including dehydration, lack of fiber, holding the need to poop for long periods of time, not enough exercise, diarrhea, and vomiting. More serious causes of constipation are intestinal obstructions, diabetes, irritable bowel syndrome, anal fissures, and more. It is important to talk to your child's doctor if she regularly experiences constipation.

Preventing constipation

The best way to prevent constipation is by making sure your child eats a balanced diet high in fiber. A variety of things can cause constipation, but a diet low in fiber and high in processed foods can make a child more susceptible. Reduce the amount of processed foods and foods high in sugar that your child eats on a daily basis. Increase the amount of high-fiber foods your child eats. Also, make sure your child gets regular physical activity. Encourage your child to drink plenty of water. Staying fully hydrated can help prevent constipation. Make sure your child is not ignoring the need to poop or delaying it. Holding poop in for too long can cause constipation. Finally, avoid letting your child take stimulant laxatives; these can cause physical dependency and lead to more serious intestinal problems in the future. For constipation, you only should give your child medicine recommended or prescribed by a doctor. If your child frequently gets constipated, you should bring it up with your child's doctor.

Treating constipation

In the majority of cases, constipation is a temporary situation that will clear up with simple lifestyle changes. Similar to the suggestions for preventing constipation, switching your child to a high-fiber diet, increasing water drinking, and getting more physical activity will help treat constipation. If these lifestyle changes do not work, your child's doctor might suggest a fiber supplement, such as FiberCon or Citrucel, a child-safe laxative, or a stool softener. If these over-the-counter treatments do not work, prescription medicines are available, and medical procedures may be needed if the constipation is being caused by a blockage. If the constipation has resulted in impacted stool, a serious medical condition in which the stool hardens to the point it is impossible to push out in a regular bowel movement, surgical removal might be necessary.

It is important to consult your child's doctor if she is regularly experiencing constipation, or if the constipation has not cleared up after making changes to her diet and activity level. Constipation can lead to a number of other problems including hemorrhoids, fissures, stool impaction, and a condition called rectal prolapse, which occurs when rectal tissue gets pushed up against the anus and causes secretion.

Consoling during constipation

Constipation can make pooping uncomfortable and often painful. Help your child get through it by telling her you know it hurts. Sit with her in the bathroom while she tries to poop. Make sure she drinks plenty of water and eats foods high in fiber. It is important to help your child relax while trying to poop. While she is sitting on the toilet, you can read to her, tell jokes, talk, or sing songs. The more relaxed she is, the easier it will be for her to poop. Do not let constipation go on for too long before contacting a doctor. The faster constipation is cleared up, the better your toddler will feel.

Pushing too hard, which causes tearing

If your child is having a hard time pooping, she is likely trying to push hard to make the poop come out. However, pushing too hard can cause tearing, which can make pooping hurt even more, and it can make your child more susceptible to an infection. This tearing is referred to as fissures. Fissures are like little paper cuts or cracks on her anus. In addition to being painful, fissures also can lead to an infection because they are not easy to keep clean. If your child does experience tearing, make sure to wipe for her after she poops. Make sure her bottom is completely clean after each time she sits on the toilet. When you take her to see her doctor, make sure to tell the doctor about the fissures.

Once again, a diet high in fiber will help make pooping easier for your child so she is not tempted to push hard. Relaxing while she poops will make pooping easier and relieve the need for pushing hard. Adding fiber to your child's diet can solve pooping problems gradually and naturally. It can make pooping easier and more comfortable for your child. Many foods are naturally high in fiber and are easily added to your child's diet. In addition to adding higher fiber foods, you also can decrease highly processed foods that are often harder to digest. If your child is having problems pooping, you should attempt to avoid or decrease the amount of premade and fast food your child consumes.

Foods high in fiber

- ☆ Oatmeal
- ☆ Shredded wheat
- ☆ Granola
- ☆ Raisin bran
- ☆ Bran muffins
- ☆ Whole grain bagels or English muffins
- ☆ Brown rice
- ☆ Whole wheat pasta
- ☆ Barley
- ☆ Wild rice
- ☆ Peas
- ☆ Beans
- ☆ Broccoli
- ☆ Cauliflower
- ☆ Figs
- ☆ Blueberries
- ☆ Apples with the skin on

Uncircumcised Boys

Boys are born with a piece of skin, called the foreskin, covering the head of the penis. Circumcision is a procedure that removes the foreskin so the head of the penis is constantly exposed. This procedure typically is performed during the baby's first ten days. When done in this early stage of life, it can be done at the hospital or by your pediatrician or family doctor. In some cases, a religious official performs the procedure. Between 55 and 65 percent of baby boys born in the United States are circumcised. Circumcision is more common in the United States, Canada, and the Middle East than in other areas like Asia, South and Central America, and Europe.

Uncircumcised boys still have the foreskin attached to their penises, covering the head of the penis. Although eventually the foreskin will be able to retract completely, exposing the head of the penis, 96 percent of newborns do not have retractable foreskins. Typically, by the time the boy is 1 year old, the foreskin will retract about 50 percent, and by age 3, the foreskin should be able to retract completely. The inability of the foreskin to retract completely until age 3 creates a cleanliness issue that needs to be dealt with carefully.

Infections in uncircumcised boys

The existence of the foreskin, especially when it is not able to completely retract, creates an environment that is susceptible to the growth of bacteria and infections. A condition called balanitis is the inflammation of the glands caused by a buildup of bacteria under the foreskin. Balanitis can cause painful swelling and difficulty peeing. In extreme cases, balanitis only can be treated with circumcision.

Uncircumcised boys are also at a greater risk of developing a urinary tract infection and bacteria-related infections, which makes teaching cleanliness during potty training increasingly important.

When an uncircumcised boy gets an infection, it is important to bring the boy to the doctor instead of trying to treat it yourself. These types of infections can become painful and lead to other problems. It is important to treat them quickly and professionally. The pain of an infection and the fear of peeing can derail your potty training efforts.

Extra cleaning

In order to clean an uncircumcised boy properly, you need to push back the foreskin gently as far as it will retract. Stop as soon as you feel resistance. Once you have done this, clean the entire exposed area of the penis. When you let go, the foreskin will go back over the head of the penis. The point of this is to make sure no bacteria from the urine stays on the head of the penis and is trapped between the skin of the penis and the foreskin. Bacteria in this area are what lead to balanitis and urinary tract infections. It is important to do this every time you change his diaper. Once he starts potty training, either you or he needs to do this every time he pees.

Teaching the boy to take care of his privates

When you first start potty training, continue to clean your son's foreskin area yourself, but explain to him what you are doing and why. Then, have him clean the area with you there instructing him. Unless you are practicing early potty training, his foreskin should be completely retractable by the time you are potty training. Show him how to pull back the foreskin, wipe the penis clean, and then, allow the foreskin to go back into place. Due to the risk of infection, it is important that he learn to clean himself at a young age. Continue monitoring his self-cleaning, and offer instruction or advice when needed. Anytime he is going to be away from you, such as at preschool or with a caregiver, remind him to clean himself every time he uses the potty. When he is bathing, check for any redness or swelling. The sooner an infection is identified, the quicker it can be dealt with.

Diabetes

Roughly, 13,000 kids are diagnosed with Type 1 Diabetes each year. When a child has diabetes, the excess glucose leaves the body through urine. This causes the child to pee frequently. If your child seems constantly thirsty, pees excessively throughout the day, and regularly cannot make it through the night without going to the bathroom, you should see the child's doctor. This is a high indicator for diabetes, and the sooner it is discovered, the better. Children with diabetes also may have an increased problem with bed-wetting. If this is the case, frequently remind your child that it is not her fault. Provide her with pull-ups to alleviate the embarrassment of a mess.

Vulvovaginitis

Vulvovaginitis is an infection caused by gut bacteria, which is found in poop, being transferred to the vagina. Vulvovaginitis causes swelling, soreness, and itchiness. It can make it painful for your daughter to pee. Although it is possible for infant girls to develop this type of infection, it is not as common because parents typically change their daughter's diaper soon after she has pooped. When a girl is going through potty training, the infection can develop because of ineffective or improper wiping. If your daughter is wiping herself from back to front, she is spreading all the germs from her poop over her vagina. It is very important that you teach your daughter to wipe front to back, and to make sure she is completely clean after wiping herself. The average girl cannot effectively wipe herself until age four or five.

Another contributing factor in the development of this condition is scratching. It is common once girls stop wearing diapers to frequently scratch themselves. This is, in part, due to the difference in feel between the diaper and the big girl underwear. Many girls will scratch themselves in their sleep without even being aware of the fact they are scratching. Scratching can make the skin around the vagina raw, which will make it easier for an infection to develop.

If your daughter develops a red and itchy rash on or around her vagina, take her to the doctor. The doctor can prescribe a topical antibiotic that will help clear up the infection quickly. Help stop the infection from reoccurring by making sure she is properly wiping herself after each bathroom visit. Finally, having your daughter bathe daily will help wash away any fecal matter or bacteria that may have been left behind during wiping.

Thrush

Thrush is a fungal infection that can also cause a red and itchy rash. Unlike vulvovaginitis, which is not commonly seen in children over the age of eight, thrush can develop at any age. It develops and spreads in warm, damp conditions. Thrush also results in a thick white discharge. If you think your daughter has developed thrush, take her to see her doctor. It is easily treatable with medication. Thrush can reoccur easily, so it is important to take the medication as long as the doctor recommends, not just until the symptoms disappear. Finally, having your daughter wear cotton underwear will help decrease the chances of developing thrush. Cotton underpants will help keep her cooler.

Chapter 13:
Potty Training Under Special Circumstances

There are a variety of special circumstances in which the typical rules or methods of potty training cannot be applied. Some of these situations include training children with learning disabilities or potty training multiples. These circumstances may change the method you use, the tactics you employ to make the methods successful, or the age you initiate potty training. As in other situations, it is important to make potty training decisions based on the child you are potty training because every child is different. It is important to be flexible and maintain a positive outlook. No matter what the situation is, there is a potty training solution.

Learning Disabilities

Although not all learning disabilities will affect potty training directly, it is important to choose a potty training method that will match your child's unique learning style. For example, some children will learn faster and better when they are able to learn through books and videos with pictures and images of what they need to be doing instead of verbal instruction being the main form of teaching. For children with moderate to severe learning disabilities, it is important to discuss potty training with the child's doctor to ensure you are not placing unattainable expectations on your child. There are preferred methods to follow when teaching children with attention deficit disorder, attention deficit hyperactivity disorder, Down syndrome, and autism.

CASE STUDY: POTTY
TRAINING CHILDREN WITH
HEARING IMPAIRMENTS

B. Spenser

I have one boy and one girl. Both of my children were born deaf, and they have both had cochlear implants. We went through a lot when they were infants and toddlers because of the surgeries, the speech therapist, all the doctors, and more. We made the decision to hold off potty training until they were a little older. Both of the children were three when we potty trained them. By doing this, the children were able to communicate with us. We also were able to talk to them and know they understood what we were explaining to them. We kept the process simple, and we used a sticker chart to reward bowel movements. We did use a potty chair, which doubled as a footstool, so they could easily wash their hands at the sink. I do not believe my experience with potty training was any more difficult because of the children's hearing impairment.

ADD and ADHD

Some of the primary problems faced by parents trying to potty train a child with ADD or ADHD are getting the child to focus on the task, to identify the feelings of needing to go to the bathroom, and to relax long enough for his body to pee or poop as needed. In order to potty train a child, a parent needs to be able to explain to the child how and when to use the potty. In this situation, it is best to use stress-free methods that do not require long periods of training. Intensive methods, such as the one-day method, are going to be more than your child can handle. Focusing on small but clear training sessions will help your child focus for a short amount of time. When leading up to initiating potty training, read many potty storybooks, and have your child repeatedly watch potty training videos if he is willing to sit through them. Find videos that are short and have vivid colors and imagery.

Before initiating potty training, talk to your child's doctor. Have your child's doctor help you determine the right age to start, if you are unsure. If your doctor is accustomed to working with kids with ADD or ADHD, he or she might even have specific advice for you that has worked for other patients. Finally, seek the support of other parents raising children with ADD or ADHD. Having support from other parents can help you get through the process with minimal stress and anxiety. Just as with other kids, hostility or irritation from parents can impede the potty training process.

CASE STUDY: POTTY TRAINING A CHILD WITH ATTENTION DEFICIT HYPERACTIVITY DISORDER

Matt Harkins

My oldest was diagnosed with ADHD at a young age. By the time he was two, he was no longer taking naps, he was on the move all day long, he would even throw up while eating because he could not sit still. After he was diagnosed as hyperactive, I cut all sugar and many artificial dyes and sweeteners to help the situation, but he was still constantly in motion. He had a hard time focusing on anything for more than a couple of minutes, sometimes even less. I worked with a child development specialist to help me get him through the normal developmental milestones, but everything was a struggle.

The primary problems I had with potty training were getting him to realize when he needed to go and getting him to sit on the toilet long enough to go. He would often jump of the toilet while peeing, which resulted in a mess, or he would run out of the bathroom before actually going and then have an accident. I developed strategies to deal with these problems separately. I kept track of when I knew he normally used the bathroom, and started taking him to the bathroom at regular times instead of waiting for him to tell me. I also did not ask him if he needed to go, I just took his hand and walked him to the bathroom. I also paid attention to when he ate and drank and took him to the bathroom within about a half an hour of him eating and drinking. I figured if I kept taking him to the bathroom, at least he would not be having accidents or staying in diapers. Eventually, he did catch on to the feelings of needing to go, and started going on his own.

The second problem I dealt with by first having him take a deep breath when he sat on the toilet. This would give him a moment of sitting still to let his body relax and release the pee. After he took the deep breath, I would have him sing a song with me, and he had to sit on the toilet for the entire song. If he started peeing during the song, I would keep it going. Then, after the song, I would ask him if he had any more pee in his body that needed to come out. I had to go in the bathroom with him every time to do this in order to make sure he sat on the toilet. I did this for several weeks. Even after he was reliably dry, I had to remind him each time to sit there for more than a second. I still was going with him to the bathroom regularly until he started school. I was extremely nervous sending him to school, but it turned out OK. He did not have any accidents, and his teacher said he did go when instructed to during bathroom breaks.

Down syndrome

Potty training a child with Down syndrome can take anywhere from a couple of months to more than a year. It is important to start by helping your child realize the difference between being wet and being dry, as well as identifying how it feels to need to pee and poop. This will need to be accomplished before you will be able to explain what to do in the bathroom.

This is the first step because without this understanding, your child will be unable to identify the need to go or make a connection between his wet pants and his need to pee. One way you can do this is by using the doll method described in the one-day potty training method. Although you will not be able to potty train a child with Down syndrome in one day, you still can use the same technique over a longer period. Dr Azrin and Dr. Foxx, who initially developed the one-day method, came up with it based on techniques used when teaching disabled children. The idea behind potty training a doll is that children will learn faster through the process of teaching. Another way to help your child make the connection is to start checking your child's diaper regularly. If he is wet, say, "wet." If he is dry, say, "dry." Do this several times throughout the day. Do this every time you change his diaper, in the morning and in the evening. Continue doing this for several days. Then, before announcing whether he is wet or dry, ask him if he is wet or dry. If he answers correctly, reward him by smiling and telling him he is right. If he is incorrect or does not answer, move on by saying either "wet" or "dry."

You also want to make him aware that people go pee and poop in the potty. Take him in the bathroom with you. Point to the toilet and say "potty" every time. This will help him to connect the word "potty" with the toilet. Second, each time you go in the bathroom, tell him you either "need to pee" or "need to poop." Do this every time you go to the bathroom. This will help him make a connection between the words and the actions. Reading potty storybooks and watching potty training videos also will help reinforce these lessons. The more you talk about the bathroom, peeing, pooping, and the need to go, the more opportunities your child will have to understand and remember what you are saying. Repetition is key for all children, and children with Down syndrome are no different.

Once you feel he is starting to make the connection between the words and what they mean, start having him sit on the potty at regular times throughout the day. Although you should not force him to sit on the potty if he is resisting, you can encourage him to sit on the potty by making it fun. Stay in the bathroom with him and talk, sing, read books, or tell jokes. Do what ever it takes to encourage him to stay on the potty. He does not have to go potty while sitting there. Have him pull his pants down and sit on the toilet for a couple of minutes. While he is sitting there, ask him if he needs to pee or poop. Regardless of his answer or whether he actually pees or poops on the potty, reward him with a smile and congratulations for sitting on the potty so nicely. Once he is used to sitting on the potty several times throughout the day, start coordinating his drink times so he is likely to need to pee during a regular potty break.

When your child has peed in the potty for the first time, reward him by telling him what a great job he did. Then, help him wipe himself and pull his pants back up. Explain to him what needs to be done at each step. Continue this routine until he is regularly going during the scheduled potty breaks. It is important to be positive and supportive even if he does not use the potty during a schedule potty break. It is important not to make him feel like he failed or disappointed you. If he is unable to go or completes a step incorrectly, do not reprimand him. Just redirect him to the correct way of doing things. Talk him through using the potty each time.

Autism

Potty training children with autism can be different in a number of ways. First, children with autism may start potty training at a later age, or it may take longer to potty train them depending on the severity of their autism. Even after potty training is complete, it still might be important to accompany your child to the bathroom. Even if he now knows the steps of going potty, he might need ongoing guidance or direction.

The best approach for potty training children with autism is often the use of sequential picture cards. Create cards that have pictures and words for each step of using the potty. The cards do not need to be greatly detailed. They can be made with photos, clip art on the computer, drawings, or magazine cutouts. If you want to make it really personalized, you can include pictures of your child flushing the toilet or washing his hands. Each time you take your child to the bathroom, show him the card that coordinates with the needed action, say the command aloud, and then, help him complete the action. For example, if the first card instructs him to pull down his pants, then you will want to show him the card, tell him to pull down his pants, and then, help him do it. Go through this process every time you take him into the bathroom. Repetition will help him learn the steps needed to go to the bathroom, and it will help him adjust to the transition from diapers to underwear.

Parents of autistic children might encounter a variety of common problems when potty training. One is the child's resistance to change. Although all children may resist the transition out of diapers, autistic children are more likely to resist the entire process. They may resist the change in routine, the change from diapers to underwear, the sounds or feel of the bathroom, the coldness of the toilet seat, or the sound of the flushing toilet. If you are experiencing resistance from your child, it is important to discover the source of the resistance and then deal specifically with that problem.

Another common problem encountered when potty training autistic children is the child's tendency to repeat actions. For example, it is common for a child to flush the toilet repeatedly after using the potty. One way to deal with this is to use the sequential picture cards. Once your child is potty trained, have him take the cards with him each time he uses the potty, and teach him to flip the card over after he completes the task. This way, when he sees the flush card, he will flush the toilet and then flip to the next card. This will take him to the next action.

If your child sees a counselor, you should let the counselor know you are initiating potty training. The counselor may have some helpful advice for you because the counselor already will know your child. You also should talk to your child's doctor and teachers if your child is already in school, because absolute consistency in routine is important. If the teachers are aware of your potty training efforts, they can keep you updated on any accomplishments or changes in behavior that happen while your child is at school.

CASE STUDY: POTTY TRAINING A CHILD WITH ASPERGER'S SYNDROME

Sara White

I have five boys and one on the way. My oldest son has Asperger's syndrome. However, he was not diagnosed until after he started school. Although I knew we were having problems, I did not realize he had an actual problem. Being my first child, I did not realize what we were going through was different than normal first child experiences. When he was two years old, I decided to potty train him. I took him out of diapers and introduced him to the potty. I started out determined because I was set mentally to have him potty trained quickly. He did not respond to potty training well at all. He did not want to make the transition, and he completely fought the entire process.

I ended up backing off and letting him go back into diapers. He refused even to approach the potty again until he was four years old. My fast and determined approach completely scared him away from the bathroom. Once again, at the time, I still did not know he had Asperger's syndrome. I have learned a great deal about Asperger's over the years, and I know now that I should have taken a significantly softer approach to potty training.

With my next three boys, I waited until they were well past two before starting potty training because I did not want to scare any of them away from using the potty. Even though I am now aware of why my first potty training experience went so badly, I found that waiting until the boys were a little older was significantly easier. It was easier to communicate with them, and being old enough to talk allowed the boys to communicate their needs better with me. I have one more boy still in diapers and one on the way, and I plan to take the same approach with them.

Potty Training Multiplies

Potty training multiple children at one time can be intimidating. The important thing to remember is that you are potty training individual children. Your multiples may not all be ready to potty train at the same time. It is important to find a method of potty training that will work for you while still considering your children's unique personalities. If you have boy/girl twins, potty training them separately will make the process easier. The physical differences will make it hard to potty train them together while still teaching them the things they need to learn individually.

Whether you potty train multiples at the same time or individually, you may need help separating the children. A close friend or family member can assist in entertaining one child while you are in the bathroom with the other. This will prevent the children from being distracted by each other during potty training. Seeking support and help from mothers of multiples groups also will aid in the potty training process. Potty training multiples does not need to be any more difficult than potty training a singleton. As long as you are mentally prepared and go into it with a positive attitude, your toddlers will respond favorably.

Twin Training: A Story from the Author

It was clear from the time my girls were only a few months old that they had very different personalities. As they learned to crawl, walk, and talk, it became clear that although Katelyn attempted everything first, Allison mastered it first because she tended to take her time to figure out the best way to do things.

In this photo, older sister Natalie is showing Allison how to use the potty doll.
PHOTO COURTESY OF MELANIE WILLIAMSON

I made one brief attempt to potty train the girls together using the same method, but I quickly realized it was not going to work for us.

I then decided to use their personality differences to my advantage. I encouraged both girls to use the potty, but I really focused on Allison. As I expected, Allison figured out what was expected of her and what she needed to do faster. She was the first to pee and poop in the potty, and she was the first to start announcing when she needed to go instead of waiting for me to ask her. However, Katelyn's naturally competitive spirit drove her to achieve all the same accomplishments Allison did. While Allison learned by listening to me, Katelyn learned by watching Allison. In addition, when Allison had an accident she would take her clothes off on her own and leave them in the bathroom. When Katelyn had an accident, she would cry and insist I come help her. Katelyn proved to be far more sensory-orientated than Allison. Allison proved to have more of an internalizing temperament. Each time she had an accident, she would ask me if she was still a good girl.

Potty training Allison and Katelyn made me realize how important it will be to acknowledge their differences as they get older. It is very easy with twins to treat them the same and involve them in the same activities because they are the same age. However, twins can be as different as any two siblings. Even though they will always have the unique bond of being twins, they always will be two very different and distinct people, and going through potty training with them helped me realize that.

Higher order multiples

Higher order multiples are triplets, quadruplets, and more. Higher order multiples also sometimes are referred to as super twins. As with twins, it is important to remember that higher order multiples are still distinctly different children. Recognizing their differences likely will provide you an advantage in potty training. Attempting to potty train them at the same time may be the easiest approach. In addition to learning from you, they will learn from each other.

CASE STUDY: POTTY TRAINING TRIPLETS

K. Majewski

We have triplets, two girls and one boy. We also have a boy slightly older than the triplets. I was very anxious about the thought of potty training the triplets because I just kept thinking about how crazy it was going to be trying to potty train all of them while still caring for our older son. My husband works during the day, so the brunt of the work was going to fall on me. I knew from potty training our older son that being prepared was going to be my best tactic. I bought lots of big kid underwear and three potty chairs. I figured if I had one for each child, then I would not have to worry about running around to multiple bathrooms if the kids all had to go at the same time.

I took different approaches with potty training. First, I scheduled family potty breaks, which were when we woke up, after each meal / snack, and right before bed. During the family potty break, I would have all four kids go in the bathroom to go potty together. I would go in the bathroom with them and sit on the floor. I did this so the triplets could see that their big brother had to go potty, too. In addition, the kids commonly had to go pee anyway during these times of the day, so I figured it would inspire early successes.

The second approach I took was having the kids dressed as little as possible. Although I was not completely comfortable with having the kids run around naked, I allowed them to wear just a t-shirt and underwear. Several parents I know went with the naked approach, but with triplets, I just thought that was too many naked kids at once. Because we used regular underwear, it was immediately obvious when one of them peed; so I got the same results as letting them go naked. They did not all get it at the same time, but the method did work. It took about two months, but all three kids regularly went without accidents during the day. Once I was confident they were all fully potty trained, we went out for ice cream to celebrate.

Chapter 14:
Continuing the Potty Training

Although your major goal is to have your toddler reliably dry throughout the day, and ideally at night, potty training does not end once this is accomplished. Other potty-related lessons, both big and small, will need to be addressed. These include transitioning your son from peeing sitting down to peeing standing up, transitioning to an adult toilet, dealing with accidents at school, talking about problems without embarrassment, and understanding privacy. Good hygiene also will be an ongoing lesson for most toddlers.

Teaching Boys to Pee Standing Up

Although teaching a boy to pee sitting down is best during potty training, your son will need to learn how to pee standing up. He can begin peeing while standing as soon as he is fully potty trained and is tall enough to aim into the toilet. If you are still using the potty chair, this will not be a problem.

Learning to pee standing up involves learning the mechanics of the position, how to aim correctly, and not to be afraid. One of the primary differences between peeing sitting down and peeing standing up is his pants. To pee sitting down, he pulled his pants and underwear completely down. Now he will need to learn to pee while still holding up his pants and underwear. The best way to learn this is direct instruction from an older male. If the boy's father is unavailable, this can be another trusted male relative who is comfortable with the assignment. Similarly to other potty training lessons, this lesson should be done step by step. Allow him to see other males peeing while standing. Have him read potty books and watch potty videos that show boys peeing while standing. Another good way is to let him stand in the backyard to pee. He will have to keep his pants on, but he can have fun aiming at bushes as he learns.

The second part of learning to pee while standing is learning how to aim. When a little boy does not know how to aim the pee into the toilet, it is likely to go all over himself and the floor. You can purchase flushable pee targets from baby-supply stores. You can also use small cereal such as Cheerios®. Drop a couple into the toilet and instruct your toddler to try to hit the Cheerios with his pee. This method is fun for your toddler and is likely to engage him.

Finally, you need to teach your son not to be afraid. This particularly applies to public restrooms. Public men's rooms typically have urinals or troths, as opposed to toilets. They also do not provide the privacy of a bathroom at home. This can be intimidating for a little boy. The first key is to have him go into the bathroom with a trusted male for the first several months or even years after being potty trained, depending on the age your child is potty trained. Having someone he knows nearby will decrease the fear. Second, talking about his fears frequently will help dissipate them.

Transitioning to an Adult Toilet

Moving to an adult toilet can be scary for a child accustomed to a potty chair. Your toddler may be afraid of falling in or off the toilet. One way to make the transition easier is to go from a potty chair to a potty seat first, and then to the toilet without a potty seat. The potty seat will help your toddler adjust to the height of the toilet and how to get on it. Public toilets can be particularly scary because, often, the toilet seat is significantly larger than home toilet seats. In this case, it may be best to go in the stall with your toddler and keep your hands on her waist as she goes so she feels more secure. In most cases, children are eager to use the same toilet the big people use, and the transition is seamless.

Older Child Regression

Occasionally, older children will regress back to not being potty trained or having frequent accidents. This refers to children who have been solidly potty trained for more than a year. This is typically the result of a serious disruption in the child's life. It can include a traumatic event, the loss of a close loved one, or it can be a sign of abuse. If you have an older child that regresses, it is important to see the child's doctor first to rule out a medical problem or a sexual or physical abuse problem. Depending on the source of the problem or if the source of the problem is even known, you may need to take your child to see a professional counselor. This should be someone who specializes in children. If the regression is the result of a loved one, see a counselor who specializes in grief counseling. If the regression is the result of abuse, see a counselor that specializes in abuse. Whatever the discovered reason is, find a counselor specially trained to handle the situation.

Accidents at school

Occasionally, a school-aged child may have an accident. If the accident was random and isolated, it is not likely to be connected to a larger issue. The accident may be a result of the child being distracted, waiting too long before going, or being unable to get undressed fast enough. To avoid school accidents, regularly talk to your child about not waiting until the last second to go. Make sure your child always is wearing clothes she can get in and out of quickly. Young school-aged children, such as those in kindergarten and first grade, should avoid wearing jeans with buttons. They can be difficult to get undone quickly, and that may lead to an accident.

If your child does have an accident, assure her that it was just an accident, and it was not her fault. She is likely to be highly embarrassed, so it is important to minimize the accident. Make sure no one in the family, especially other siblings, brings it up, makes jokes about the accident, or makes fun of her for having one. Talk to her about the accident to see what the cause was, and work to avoid that particular cause in the future.

If, for any reason, you are concerned your child may have an accident at school, leave an extra pair of clothes for your child in the nurse's office, with the teacher, or in your child's locker. Being prepared is always the best strategy, and you can leave extra clothes at the school without all your child's classmates knowing why.

Talking about Bathroom Problems

When your baby has constipation, diarrhea, or a rash, it is easy to address it quickly because you are aware of the problem immediately. Once your child is potty trained, you are unlikely to become aware of the problem unless it gets very bad or your child tells you. To prevent problems from escalating, it is important to encourage your child to tell you about problems right away. Do not make jokes about the problem or blow it off. You do not want your child to be too embarrassed to tell you anything in the future. Do not tell other people about your child's bathroom problem. It may seem innocent to tell your mother that your child is constipated, but if your mother then mentions it to her grandchild, the child will be aware that you were talking about something behind her back. This may cause embarrassment, anger, or even distrust. The older your child is, the more negatively she is likely to respond to you telling other family members.

In addition to eliminating or decreasing embarrassment, you want to make sure your child understands how to describe the problem. Explain to your child what constipation feels like. If your child feels sick, have her describe how she feels, and then, ask her pointed questions to learn more. For example, if you are concerned your daughter might have a UTI, ask her if it burns a lot when she pees, or if she has sharp pains between or below her hip bones in her lower abdomen.

Teaching Privacy

Privacy can be difficult to teach during potty training because you are always in the bathroom with your child while she tries to go. However, once your child is potty trained, it is important that she understands what privacy is and its importance. Start by simply instructing her to close the bathroom door while she is in there. Each time you do, tell her the bathroom is private, and other people should not be able to see her while she goes potty. Repeatedly tell her exactly which people are allowed to see her while she is going potty. This should be a limited number of trusted adults, such as parents or parents and the babysitter. The people allowed in the bathroom will vary depending on your child's situation.

Talk to her about the importance of privacy at school and in public bathrooms. Remind her that no one should follow her into a bathroom or open the door while she is in there. Although you do not want to scare her, repeatedly reminding her of these things will help her protect herself. She will know something is wrong if an unapproved person tries to go in the bathroom with her. Each time you talk about it, tell her if this happens, she should go find you, or her caregiver, depending on where she is at the time.

It is also important to teach her that other people need privacy, too, so she cannot go in the bathroom or open the door if other people are in there. This may be confusing at first because you encouraged her to be in the bathroom with other people during potty training. However, once she is potty trained, you need to start teaching privacy. One way to reinforce this is to start turning around or having her turn around. For example, if you and your daughter go into a public restroom room, turn around when it is her turn to pee. Tell her you are turning around because her going pee is private. Likewise, when it is your turn to pee, ask her to turn around, so you can have privacy.

Using a Public Bathroom Alone

Allowing your child to go into a public bathroom alone is big step for you and your child. The best way to ease into this is by taking baby steps. For example, allow your child to go into a stall alone and stand outside the stall in case she needs help. Allow her to go in a single public bathroom alone. After you are sure she can handle using the toilet alone, allow her to go into the stall alone without you standing right outside the stall door. Tell her to call for you if she needs help.

As you get more comfortable with her using a public bathroom, you can stand outside the bathroom door and let her go in by herself. When she comes out, ask her if she remembered to wipe, flush, and wash her hands. If you are in a new place, check the bathroom first for cleanliness or other exits that may confuse your child. If a public bathroom ever makes you feel nervous, go with her, but assure her it is not because you do not trust her to go on her own. Always accompany your child if it is a large bathroom with multiple exits like in an airport or sport stadium.

The issue of letting your child go into a public bathroom alone often becomes an issue earlier when parents are dealing with a child of the opposite sex. A little boy may want to stop going in the women's room with his mother well before his mother is OK with him going into the men's room alone. There are a variety of ways to handle this situation depending on where you are and the size of the public bathroom. How you deal with it may also depend on what you are most worried about. If you are concerned about your child being in a bathroom alone with strangers, you can call into the bathroom first to see if it is empty. Then, let your son into the bathroom, but stand right outside the bathroom door and wait for him. If a particular bathroom makes you too nervous, you can always leave and find somewhere else to go, or take your child into the bathroom with you. Your child may not be happy, but if you feel the situation is not safe, then it is the best solution.

Chapter 15:
Life Lessons Learned Through Potty Training Your Child

Because potty training can be stressful, it is a great way to reveal how you will parent under pressure. For example, you might realize you are quick to lose your temper when your child has an accident. Although this revelation may disturb you, revealing it will give you the opportunity to change it. Likewise, potty training might teach you that you are far more patient and optimistic than you give yourself credit for. You might realize you have many creative ideas that solve problems in the moment. Most potty training methods were developed by parents who were faced with a problem they could not find a solution to. The creator of the potty party threw her son a potty party out of desperation because the preschool her son attended made it clear he needed to be potty trained.

Potty training is a tremendous experience for both parents and children. It either can be a positive experience or a negative one depending on how it is approached by parents and caregivers. Throughout the process, parents will be presented with the opportunity to demonstrate qualities such as patience, kindness, and understanding. You also will be presented with the opportunity to spend an increased amount of time with your child. You can choose to appreciate that extra time and spend it bonding with your child.

Patience

You need to have patience to potty train your toddler successfully. Children cannot go on command, and if they feel rushed, they might not be able to go at all. It is also important to be patient with them when they have accidents. Potty training is a learning process and a big transition for your little one. Patience is defined as an ability and willingness to suppress annoyance when facing delays and a steady perseverance. This means not losing your temper when things are not going the way you thought they would, and being OK with just sitting with your toddler while he tries to use the bathroom. Patience is letting him try to do things on his own.

One way you can put patience into practice is by allowing your toddler to dress himself. Learning to put clothes on the right way is a big skill for a toddler to learn, but he will learn only if he is given the opportunity to do so. It often is hard for parents to sit and wait while their toddler attempts to dress himself; it is much easier to take over and dress him quickly.

In addition to benefiting the potty training process, demonstrating patience is an essential way to teach your children the value of patience. Potty training is a difficult transition for many children, and having to deal with that in addition to constantly feeling rushed by his parents, can lead a young child to developing an impatient attitude toward life. Impatience can make the potty training process take longer than necessary and feel even longer than it actually took. Allow your children to enjoy themselves by teaching them they do not have to rush through everything.

Kindness

Young children can be sensitive and easily hurt if they feel they are being scolded for not accomplishing their goals. Even when your toddler is doing something you never want him to do again, such as playing with poop or crawling under a stall door in a public restroom, you can discourage the behavior without yelling at him or saying harsh things. Even though you might think an action is gross,

never tell your child he is gross. Remember to see things from his point of view.

Potty training is the ideal time to put kindness into practice with your child. Simply being understanding of his difficulties or accidents can be a way to show him kindness. Give him praise even when his victory is a small one. Smile, and give him plenty of hugs and attention. Children will reflect how their parents act more than what their parents verbally try to teach them. Showing your child kindness on a daily basis will teach him how to be a kind child.

Being Stern

It is important to remember that being kind does not mean letting your child do things he should not be doing or being overly lenient. You can be stern and have expectations for your child's behavior without being mean or making the punishment personal. It is important always to make sure your child knows you disapprove of his behavior, which is separate from him as a person. Punishments should not include yelling or name-calling. Focus on redirecting your child to the proper way of doing things. For example, if your child unrolls a roll of toilet paper while in the bathroom, resist the urge to get mad. Explain to the child that what he did is wasteful and not appropriate behavior. Remind him what the toilet paper is to be used for and how to use it.

Believing in Your Child

Children naturally want to make their parents proud of them. They want to earn praise and attention. Letting your child know that you believe in him and his ability to master potty training can help him to succeed. Children who do not believe in their own abilities will take longer to master a new skill because they do not have the confidence to demonstrate their new skills. However, if you regularly tell your child that you know he can do this, then he will believe he can do it, too.

As mentioned throughout the book, it is important to have a positive attitude while potting training. This is important because it will show your toddler you believe he can do this. Even though he might struggle with accidents, he will know you believe in him. This will help build his confidence, and as he grows older, he will be more willing to try new things and to work toward goals.

Showing your toddler you love him no matter what happens will lay the seeds for your future relationship with each other. A child's first experience with unconditional love should be from his parents. It will be easy to lose your temper after having to clean up mess after mess. However, not losing your temper will show your toddler that you understand he is trying his best, and you love him no matter what.

You will be spending a lot of one-on-one time with your child during this process. Do not ignore the opportunity to get to know him better. While trying to get your child to sit on the toilet, offer to read him some books or engage him in a conversation. You can tell jokes or play make believe. Although most toddlers are not old enough to understand the concept of telling a joke, it is funny listening to a toddler attempt to tell one.

Knowing What Is Best and Sticking to It

Knowing your child's temperament and personality will enable you to determine what the best potty training method will be. Once you make that decision, stick to it. You likely will have people in your life trying to tell you what to do and how to do it. You may have a child resisting your method or a caregiver unwilling to participate in the process. Regardless of the obstacles placed before you, keep moving forward. You are the parent. No one knows your child better than you do.

Some parents are in a situation in which they fear their child; they may fear their child's tantrums, violent outbursts, or inconsistent behavior. Regardless of what you actually fear in your child, the best approach you can take to potty training is consistency. Be consistent, no matter what. Even a resistant child thrives on routine in his life. He wants to know exactly what is going to happen, and that knowledge helps him mentally prepare for life. If you genuinely fear your child due to a lack of control over his behavior or outbursts, consult your child's doctor to rule out medical reasons for the uncontrollable behavior.

Remain the leader, not the follower

Although some methods allow your child to feel in control of potty training, ultimately, you need to stay in control. You need to be a leader for your child, and you need to provide your child with instruction and feedback. If you start feeling that your child is controlling the situation or testing you, you need to step back in order to regain control. One method of gaining control and promoting consistency is by using a sticker chart and prizes. Choose a prize you know your child would really look forward to. For example, it can be bowling with his dad or going swimming at the beach. Then, make a sticker chart with a picture depicting the prize your child will work toward. Give your child one sticker for each day he remains completely dry. If he knows he has to go all day without an accident in order to earn his sticker, he will be less likely to have accidents repeatedly in specific situations. For example, if your child only has accidents when the babysitter is there or when he is watching a movie, you know he is capable of using the potty but is choosing not to.

Learning Your Child's Ways

Every child is different. They have different temperaments, they learn in different ways, and they have different levels of natural confidence. Because potty training is such a significant transition in your child's life, it will force him to reveal clues to his personality. Learning to understand your child's natural inclinations will help you be a better parent. For example, in Chapter 7, you learned about the different child temperaments. Your child's temperament is something he is born with, and to some degree, it will be part of his personality for the rest of his life. A parent cannot change their child's temperament. Therefore, it is best to understand your child's temperament and learn to parent with it in mind. Doing so will increase learning, make discipline more effective, and reduce conflicts.

Learning your child's temperament will help you in a variety of ways as your child gets older. Your child's temperament will affect his learning style, personality, interests, and discipline issues. Having an understanding of your child's personality before discipline, school, and personal interests are really an issue will help prepare you as a parent. It also will give you the opportunity to learn how to deal with your child in a loving way while still allowing him to grow into his own person.

As with most things, your toddler will learn how to deal with conflict by observing you and the way you act. Potty training can be frustrating at times, and if you are quick to lose your temper, that is what you will be teaching your toddler. However, if you show your child patience, kindness, and understanding, your toddler will model those qualities as he gets older.

Observing how hard your toddler works toward becoming potty trained and achieving mastery over his ability to control himself will give you a preview of his level of determination and will. If you see that your child gives up easily, you will know your child will need you to help him build self-confidence and a positive attitude. You do not want your child continually giving up on himself as he grows up.

Potty training also will help you determine what type of learner your child is. Some people naturally learn better through verbal instruction while others learn better through visual aids and role-play. Using the potty doll and the sticker chart will allow you to see what works and what does not work with your child. This information will help you help your child as he gets older and goes through school.

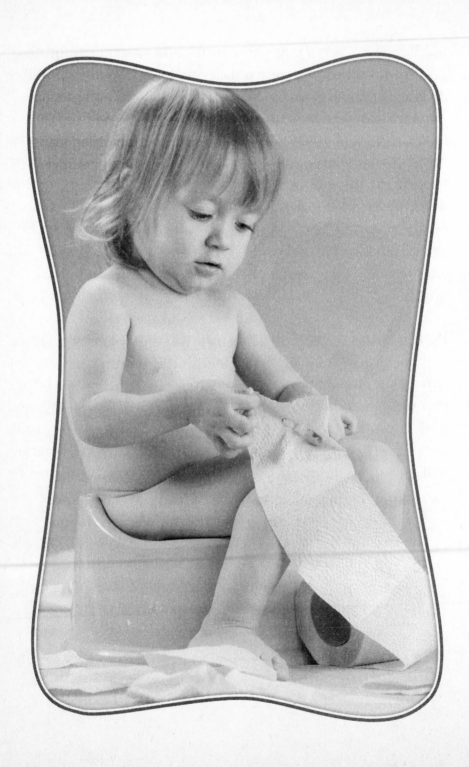

Conclusion

Potty training is a significant step in your child's life. It is one of the first major transitions that require you to work with your toddler as opposed to controlling him to ensure a successful and positive experience. There are several ongoing debates surrounding the topic of potty training. These debates include the best age to initiate potty training, the best method to choose, and the how to handle unexpected difficulties. This is why it is important to educate yourself and chose the age and methods that are best for you and your toddler.

Once you have made a decision, it is important to be confident and stick with your decision. Your attitude going into potty training can make all the difference in the world. Your toddler will notice your underlying emotions, so if you go into potty training with doubts and fears, it will affect your child's success. Do not let other parents tell you that what you are doing is wrong. Every child is different, and every child will respond to potty training differently.

Have fun with the process. Potty training provides a unique opportunity for you to spend one-on-one time with your child, and that is rare for many parents. Spend time reading potty books, playing games, and watching potty videos together. Talk to your child about using the potty and how he feels about it. Ask him lots of questions. Often, when a child is curious, nervous, or scared about something, he will tell you, if given the opportunity.

Finally, be prepared. Be prepared when you start potty training, be prepared for accidents, and be prepared to talk about body parts and potty activity. The better prepared you are, the better off you will be. Being prepared for accidents will help decrease the embarrassment for your toddler, and it will enable you to handle the situation quickly and without significant turmoil. Keep wipes and extra clothes in each of your vehicles. This will prevent the need for emergency trips home. And good luck!

Potty Training Supply Lists

One-Day Method Checklist

- ❑ Party decorations
- ❑ Potty chair or seat
- ❑ Potty doll
- ❑ Potty doll clothes
- ❑ Fake pee
- ❑ Fake poop
- ❑ Beverages
- ❑ Small wrapped gifts
- ❑ Sticker chart for potty doll
- ❑ Sticker chart for toddler
- ❑ Books
- ❑ Videos
- ❑ Timer
- ❑ Potty tracking chart
- ❑ Hand soap
- ❑ Stool to reach the sink

AAP Method Checklist

- ❑ Stickers
- ❑ Sticker chart
- ❑ Potty chair or seat
- ❑ Underwear
- ❑ Loose-fitting clothes
- ❑ Hand soap
- ❑ Stool to reach the sink

Child-Temperament Approach Checklist*

- ❑ Potty chair or seat
- ❑ Small rewards
- ❑ Temperament type questionnaire
- ❑ Books
- ❑ Videos
- ❑ Potty doll
- ❑ Day planner to keep track of potty usage
- ❑ Stool to reach the sink
- ❑ Hand soap

Stress-Free Methods Checklist*

- ❑ Potty chair or seat
- ❑ Disposable training pants
- ❑ Books
- ❑ Videos

- ❑ Potty doll
- ❑ Stickers
- ❑ Sticker chart
- ❑ Small rewards
- ❑ 30 small wrapped gifts
- ❑ Hand soap
- ❑ Stool to reach the sink

Early Potty Training Methods Checklist*

- ❑ Day planner to track potty activity
- ❑ Baby sling
- ❑ Potty pot or bowl
- ❑ Potty chair or seat
- ❑ Hand soap
- ❑ Towels for cleaning up messes

* The actual items needed will vary depending on which of the methods within that category of methods you choose to follow.

Bibliography

Azrin, N. and Foxx, R. *Toilet Training in Less Than a Day*. New York, New York: Pocket Books, 1974.

Bellis, M. "Disposable Diapers — Marion Donovan." About. com Inventors. **http://inventors.about.com/od/ dstartinventions/a/Diapers.htm**.

Bouse, K. R.N. and Fitzgerald, K. M.D. "Toilet Training." University of Michigan Health System (2010). **www.med.umich.edu/yourchild/topics/toilet.htm**.

Butler, K., and Gilson, D. "A Brief History of the Disposable Diapers." *Mother Jones* (May/June 2008 issue). **www.motherjones.com/environment/2008/04/ brief-history-disposable-diaper**.

Crane, T. *Potty Train your child in Just One Day*. New York: Simon and Schuster, 2006.

Fertleman, C. and Cave, S. *Potty Train Boys the Easy Way*. Cambridge, Massachusetts: Da Capo Life Long, 2009.

Fertleman, C. and Cave, S. *Potty Train Girls the Easy Way*. Cambridge, Massachusetts: Da Capo Life Long, 2009.

Hatch, J. "The History of Potty Training in
    America." Green Baby Guide (2011).
    **http://greenbabyguide.com/2011/01/24/
    the-history-of-potty-training-in-america**.

"History of Potty Training." Potty Training Concepts (2011).
    **www.pottytrainingconcepts.com/
    A-History-of-Potty-Training.html**.

Lekovic, J. *Diaper-Free Before 3*. New York: Three Rivers Press,
    2006.

Quinn, M. "Information Center: Potty Training." Tiny Tots
    Diaper Service and Baby Boutique (2011).
    http://tinytots.com/info/potty1.html.

"Signs of Potty Training Readiness." Potty Training Concepts
    (2011). **www.pottytrainingconcepts.com/
    A-Potty-Training-Readiness-Signs.html**.

Sonna, L. *Early-Start Potty Training*. New York: McGraw Hill,
    2005.

Thomas, R. "Marion Donovan, 81, Solver of the
    Damp-Diaper problem." *New York Times* (1998).
    **www.nytimes.com/1998/11/18/business/marion-
    donovan-81-solver-of-the-damp-diaper-problem.html**.

"Washing Machine." The Great Idea Finder." (2005).
    **www.ideafinder.com/history/inventions/
    washmachine.htm**.

Wolraich, M. *Guide to Toilet Training*. New York: Bantam Books,
    2003.

Author's Bio

Although Melanie Williamson has written and published two other books, this is the book closest to her own life experiences. As the mother of three young girls, she has first-hand experience with the daily struggles of potty training. She has experienced many of the potty training issues and roadblocks she discusses in this book. Despite her struggles, she found ways to get each of her girls successfully through the potty training process. This book is the result of her personal research and experiences, as well as the experiences of several other parents.

Index

thrush 238
toilet etiquette 111
training methods
American Academy of Pediat-
   rics-recommended 29
child-temperament 29, 149
early 29
no-cry 29, 48, 53
one-day 29

U

uncircumcised boys 113,
   233, 234
UTIs 225, 228, 229

V

vasopressin 216
verbal cue 185
vulvovaginitis 49, 238

W

wiping 25, 90, 112, 113,
   115, 119, 131, 143,
   144, 189, 228, 229,
   237, 238
words referring to body
   parts 89